Programming the BeagleBone

Harness the power of BeagleBone from blinking LEDs to Internet of Things applications

Yogesh Chavan

[PACKT] open source *
PUBLISHING community experience distilled

BIRMINGHAM - MUMBAI

Programming the BeagleBone

First published: January 2016

Production reference: 1220116

Published by Packt Publishing Ltd.
Livery Place
35 Livery Street
Birmingham B3 2PB, UK.

ISBN 978-1-78439-001-3

www.packtpub.com

Cover image by Mr. Vipin Vikam (Silver photo studio, near Kasba Ganpati, Pune)

Credits

Author
Yogesh Chavan

Reviewers
Juan Cortez
Chris Desjardins
Michael Hirsch
Pavel Mamontov

Commissioning Editor
Amarabha Banerjee

Acquisition Editor
Kevin Colaco

Content Development Editor
Susmita Sabat

Technical Editor
Pranil Pathare

Copy Editor
Ting Baker

Project Coordinator
Milton Dsouza

Proofreader
Safis Editing

Indexer
Mariammal Chettiyar

Production Coordinator
Arvindkumar Gupta

Cover Work
Arvindkumar Gupta

About the Author

Yogesh Chavan is a Linux enthusiast and open source promoter, living in Pune, India. He has now been teaching operating systems, device drivers, and embedded systems in colleges and institutes for more than three years. These include the computer science department of Pune University, Symbiosis Institute of Computer Studies and Research (SICSR) college, and the Centre for Development of Advanced Computing (C-DAC) institute. He has about six years of experience in the software industry. His previous industrial role was of a software maintenance engineer at Red Hat Software Services.

Yogesh has overseen many engineering projects under GEEP (`http://www.geeksofpune.in`). He has given many talks at the annual open source event, GNUnify (`http://gnunify.in`).

Yogesh enjoys cutting edge technologies. He is a hardware hobbyist who likes playing with smartphones, tablets, routers, and Arduino. He is big fan of Android and various Linux distributions. He has compiled and modified kernel and firmwares for many phones and routers. He wishes to be a humble contributor to the open source world.

Acknowledgment

I would like to thank my wife for putting up with my late-night writing sessions. This book would not have been possible without her devotion. I would also like to give thanks and gratitude to the editors, Akash, Susmita, and Kevin, that patiently guided me. They are the source of continuous encouragement.

I would like to thank my guru Dr. Vijay Gokhale Sir, who taught me a lot more than OS. I would also like to thank my friends, Omkar Kulkarni and Ashish Shah and online friend Swiftgeek, who helped me with the electronics concepts. Also, I thank my friend, Amit Karpe, for introducing me to Packt Publishing. I thank Mrs. Nutan Chaudhari, who gave me her BeagleBone White for the purpose of testing. I used Fritzing software to draw the circuit diagrams throughout the book. I would like to thank the Fritzing team. I also thank the BeagleBoard crew for creating wonderful open source hardware boards. Finally, I would like to thank the entire open source software movement.

About the Reviewers

Juan Cortez is a first-generation college student from El Paso, Texas, majoring in electrical and computer engineering at the University of Texas at Austin. During his time in college, Juan dedicated most of his time providing services to various organizations, including the Equal Opportunity in Engineering Program, the University of Texas Longhorn Band, and Engineering Student Life. Outside of school, Juan had the distinct pleasure of interning at five different companies: Intel, Texas Instruments, Cirrus Logic, Toshiba, and IBM. In the summer of 2013, Juan interned at Texas Instruments and worked directly under the BeagleBone Black hardware architect Gerald Coley. During his time at Texas Instruments, he developed tutorials on how to program on the BeagleBone and entered their Intern Design Contest to showcase the skills that he has acquired during his internship. He is currently a software engineering intern at IBM and is working with big data by utilizing Apache Spark, which is a fast and general engine for large-scale data processing. Apart from work, Juan loves to volunteer and he mentors young students by exposing them to science, technology, engineering, and math (STEM) through fun projects and experiments.

Chris Desjardins is an embedded systems software engineer with 15 years of experience. His main focus throughout his career has been on real-time systems and multiprocessing. He has written code for a wide range of systems from small highly-parallel low power DSPs to huge real-time distributed processing systems, and everything in between. He currently loves living and working in Amsterdam, Netherlands. Look him up on LinkedIn at `http://nl.linkedin.com/in/chrisdesjardins/`

Michael Hirsch's research includes geospace remote sensing via tomography of the aurora. He has deployed autonomous outdoor climate-controlled one meter cubes with single photon sensitive cameras to rural Alaska in order to capture the faintest and fastest moving aurora that is invisible to the naked eye. He developed automatic OpenCV-based algorithms, reducing the data stream from terabytes/day to megabytes/day.

Michael founded SciVision, Inc. with applications including machine vision, embedded remote sensing systems, and wearable and batteryless sensors.

Pavel Mamontov is a Russian-born designer and web developer residing in New York City. He holds a BS degree in digital media from Drexel University and an MFA degree in design and technology from Parsons School of Design. He is currently employed at Metropolitan College of New York as an in-house web developer. In his free time, he loves to tinker with open source and open hardware technology, draw, and occasionally volunteer for various labor organizations.

www.PacktPub.com

Support files, eBooks, discount offers, and more

For support files and downloads related to your book, please visit www.PacktPub.com.

Did you know that Packt offers eBook versions of every book published, with PDF and ePub files available? You can upgrade to the eBook version at www.PacktPub.com and as a print book customer, you are entitled to a discount on the eBook copy. Get in touch with us at service@packtpub.com for more details.

At www.PacktPub.com, you can also read a collection of free technical articles, sign up for a range of free newsletters and receive exclusive discounts and offers on Packt books and eBooks.

https://www2.packtpub.com/books/subscription/packtlib

Do you need instant solutions to your IT questions? PacktLib is Packt's online digital book library. Here, you can search, access, and read Packt's entire library of books.

Why subscribe?

- Fully searchable across every book published by Packt
- Copy and paste, print, and bookmark content
- On demand and accessible via a web browser

Free access for Packt account holders

If you have an account with Packt at www.PacktPub.com, you can use this to access PacktLib today and view 9 entirely free books. Simply use your login credentials for immediate access.

Table of Contents

Preface   **vii**

Chapter 1: Cloud9 IDE   **1**

  BeagleBone hardware   **2**

    BeagleBone White (BBW)   3

    BeagleBone Black (BBB)   4

    BeagleBone Green (BBG)   5

  Installing Debian image on SD card   **5**

  Setting up BeagleBone   **7**

    Direct connection to monitor and keyboard   7

    Ethernet over USB   8

    Troubleshooting   8

    Ethernet port or USB Wi-Fi adapter   9

    Troubleshooting   9

    VNC   10

    Troubleshooting   10

    Serial Connection   10

  The bone101 page   **12**

  Cloud9 IDE   **14**

  Hello World program   **15**

    Explanation   16

  Summary   **16**

Chapter 2: Blinking Onboard LEDs   **17**

  Digital I/O   **18**

  Digital I/O functions - pinMode() and digitalWrite()   **19**

  Program to turn onboard LED ON and OFF   **20**

    Program explanation   21

Quick program to blink onboard LED	**22**
Program explanation	23
Program execution	24
Make our program better	**24**
Program explanation	25
Dancing LEDs	**26**
Program explanation	28
Dancing LEDs in both directions	**29**
Program explanation	29
Summary	**30**
Chapter 3: Blinking External LEDs	**31**
What is GPIO?	**32**
BeagleBone GPIO map	**33**
Blinking external LED circuit setup	**35**
Circuit analysis	38
Program to blink external LED	**38**
Explanation	39
Troubleshooting	39
Dancing external LEDs circuit setup	**40**
Circuit analysis	41
Program to dance external LEDs in both directions	**41**
Explanation	42
Summary	**44**
Chapter 4: Controlling LED Using a Push Button	**45**
Reading from digital components	**46**
Push button circuit setup	**46**
Circuit analysis	47
Program to read from push button	**48**
Explanation	49
Reading via interrupts	**49**
Push button LED circuit setup	**52**
Circuit analysis	53
Program to control LED by push button	**53**
Explanation	54
Summary	**54**
Chapter 5: Reading from Analog Sensors	**55**
Analog I/O	**56**
Reading from analog components	**57**
TMP36 temperature sensor circuit setup	**58**
Circuit analysis	59

Program to print temperature — 60
　Explanation — 60
LDR circuit setup — 61
　Circuit analysis — 62
Program to check light intensity — 63
　Explanation — 64
Summary — 64

Chapter 6: PWM – Writing Analog Information — 65
What is PWM? — 66
BeagleBone's PWM — 68
Writing on analog components — 69
Fading LED circuit setup — 70
Program to fade in and fade out LED — 71
　Explanation — 72
Micro servo motor circuit setup — 73
Program to control a micro servo motor — 74
　Explanation — 75
Summary — 75

Chapter 7: Internet of Things with BeagleBone — 77
Why the Internet of Things? — 78
What is the Internet of Things? — 79
Program for creating new Node.js HTTP server — 81
　HTML code — 81
　JavaScript code — 81
　Explanation — 82
　Troubleshooting — 83
Program to control an LED through web browser — 84
　HTML code — 84
　Explanation — 85
　JavaScript code — 85
　Explanation — 86
Controlling a servo motor through LAN — 87
　HTML code — 88
　JavaScript code — 88
Sending an e-mail on over-temperature — 89
　Explanation — 92
　Troubleshooting — 93
　What's next? — 93
Summary — 94

Chapter 8: Physical Computing in Python   95

Python programming in BeagleBone   **96**
Adafruit BBIO library   96
Program to blink external LEDs   **97**
Explanation   98
Program to dance external LEDs   **99**
Explanation   100
Program to read from push button   **100**
Explanation   101
    Detecting button state using interrupt   101
    Explanation   102
Program to print temperature   **102**
Explanation   103
A Program to check light intensity   **103**
Explanation   104
Program to fade in and fade out LED   **104**
Explanation   105
Program to control micro servo motor   **105**
Explanation   106
Summary   **107**

Chapter 9: UART, I2C, and SPI Programming   109

Bus and bus protocols   **110**
What is UART?   **113**
Program to read/write on UART   **115**
Explanation   117
Troubleshooting   117
I2C protocol   **118**
Program to read from ADXL345 sensor   **120**
Explanation   120
Troubleshooting   121
SPI protocol   **121**
Program to write display text on Nokia 5110 LCD   **123**
Explanation   125
Summary   **125**

Chapter 10: Internet of Things using Python   127

Flask web application framework   **128**
Installation   128
A program to display temperature remotely   **129**
Explanation   130
    Troubleshooting   130

A program to control an LED through a web browser   **131**
Explanation   132
A RESTful web app to control servo motor   **133**
Explanation   134
A program to trigger an e-mail alert on over-temperature   **135**
Explanation   137
    Troubleshooting   137
Upload server data on cloud and visualize   **137**
Explanation   139
What's next?   **140**
Security   **141**
Summary   **142**
Appendix A: GPIO Control in Bash   **143**
Explanation   **144**
Troubleshooting   **144**
Appendix B: BeagleBone Capes   **145**
Appendix C: Pinmux and the Device Tree   **147**
What is Pinmux?   **147**
What is the device tree?   **148**
Index   **149**

Preface

The whole world is moving from desktop/computers to smartphones/embedded systems. We are at the door to Internet of Things (IoT). The number of Internet connected users crossed 3.2 billion in 2015, which is almost half of the total population. The number of connected devices has exceeded the number of humans already. IoT is going to bring a combination of solutions, mixing physical world and digital world. We will interact with the digital world in newer ways than keyboard and mouse. Everyday objects will have logic in them to do their work in a better way. Multiple things will work collectively in order to achieve better results. IoT will bring lot many possibilities and opportunities along.

IoT implementation needs power-efficient embedded system solutions. There has been an exponential rise in the demand of the embedded systems in the last few years. Therefore, there is a demand for embedded programming as well. Embedded development boards such as BeagleBone play a key role here. These boards provide opportunities to new programmers to get their hands on ARM-based embedded systems. BeagleBone comes as an ultra-small, cost-effective solution with a powerful hardware that runs Debian Linux. This book tries to explore the hardware and software capabilities of BeagleBone to create real-life electronics and IoT applications quickly.

Being an open source hardware board, BeagleBone is the perfect choice to study embedded systems. Board design files and in-depth datasheets are open for being studied. It comes with an Ethernet port that allows deploying the IoT projects without making any addition to the board. It provides plenty of GPIO, ADC, UART, I2C, and SPI pins that make it the right choice for electronic projects. One can install Debian, Ubuntu, Android, and many other Liunx distributions. By default, it comes with a full-fledged Debian Linux OS running on it. This gives you all the benefits of Linux kernel such as multitasking, multiuser, and extensive device drivers support. It also allows you to do programming in many languages, including C, C++, JavaScript, Python, Ruby, Perl, and so on. This book uses BeagleBone as a tool to write useful applications on the embedded systems. Starting with the basics to set up BeagleBone and Cloud9 IDE, this book covers interfacing with various electronic components via simple programs. The electronics theory related to these components is explained in detail before using them in a program. Then, the book covers some real-life IoT applications.

This book is divided in two parts: the first part is covers programs in JavaScript and the second part of this book provides electronics projects and IoT applications in Python. Most of the physicial computing theories and concepts are covered in the JavaScript part. Programs are explained in the explanation section, immediately after it's source code. Troubleshooting steps are given wherever needed. Some programs have an execution section, which explains how a program works internally. Programming language conventions and error handling are loosely followed to make programs short and easy to understand. The language that is to be covered first is a tough choice. I choose JavaScript as it is energy-efficient, event-driven architecture. It is more suited as an IoT solution. Only sending the important information reduces the processing that is to be done on the *Thing* connected to the Internet. Javascript is a natural language of web. It comes preinstalled in the BeagleBone along with Node and Cloud9. You can start Javascript programming immediately after connecting BeagleBone. Let's start the journey of programming the BeagleBone.

What this book covers

Chapter 1, Cloud9 IDE, gives the essential information you need before you start programming on BeagleBone. It gives hardware and software-related information about the boards in the BeagleBone series. It provides you different ways to connect to BeagleBone and start Cloud9 IDE to program.

Chapter 2, Blinking Onboard LEDs, covers how to use Cloud9 IDE to write the first physical computing program—blinking onboard LED on the BeagleBone. It covers another program that creates a display pattern among the LEDs.

Chapter 3, Blinking External LEDs, explains the General Purpose Input/Output (GPIO) theory and how to attach the external LEDs to the GPIO pins. Then, it covers blinking LED and display pattern programs.

Chapter 4, Controlling LED Using a Push Button, teaches how to read from input components using polling. The interrupt method programs for each of these methods are covered.

Chapter 5, Reading from Analog Sensors, covers the theory about Analog I/O and how BeagleBone supports it. Then, it has programs to read from the TMP36 temperature sensor and light sensor.

Chapter 6, PWM – Writing Analog Information, explains how the Pulse Width Modulation (PWM) technique is used to write the analog information and how BeagleBone supports it. It has a program to fade-in LED and control the servo motor using PWM.

Chapter 7, Internet of Things with BeagleBone, explains how to implement IoT in JavaScript using BeagleBone. It covers important information about IoT. Then, there are three real-life examples. Two of them are programs to remotely control LED and servo motor. Another program is to shoot an e-mail alert when overtemperature is detected.

Chapter 8, Physical Computing in Python, explains rewriting all the programs that are covered from Chapter 3 to Chapter 6 in the Python language.

Chapter 9, UART, I2C, SPI Programming, covers popular buses in the embedded systems — UART, I2C, and SPI. All these protocols are explained here in detail. This chapter covers programs that communicate over each of these buses.

Chapter 10, Internet of Things Using Python, teaches IoT programs in Python. It has programs that were similar to the programs covered in Chapter 7. It has an additional program that uploads the temperature data over the Cloud website and we will receive the temperature graph over time for analysis.

Appendix A, GPIO Control in Bash, teaches how to set the direction and turn GPIO on/off directly by writing sysfs files.

Appendix B, BeagleBone Capes, provides information about BeagleBone add-on boards called capes.

Appendix C, Pinmux and the Device Tree, gives details about the new hardware description files that help the kernel to initialize BeagleBone. They are called device tree. It covers how to use the device tree files to select the role of the BeagleBone pin among other possibilities.

This book does not cover BeagleBone Programmable Realtime Units (PRUs) and building/customising installable image.

What you need for this book

The required hardware is as follows:

- BeagleBone Black or BeagleBone Green or BeagleBone White
- Micro SD card (4 GB+)
- One breadboard
- Ten Male-to-Male jumper wires (different colors)
- Ten LEDs
- Ten 470 Ohm resistor
- Single push button
- TMP36 sensor
- LDR
- Single 10k Ohm resistor
- Micro servo motor
- ADXL345 accelerometer module
- Nokia 5110 LCD module

The optional hardware is as follows:

- 5V 2A power adapter with 5.5 mm DC jack for BeagleBone Black and BeagleBone White (`https://www.sparkfun.com/products/12889`)
- 5V 2A micro USB power adapter for BeagleBone Green (`https://www.sparkfun.com/products/12890`)
- FTDI USB serial cable (`https://www.adafruit.com/products/70`)

Who this book is for

This book is for anyone who wants to learn programming on the embedded systems and understand key concepts such as GPIO, PWM, and bus. It is intended for a programming beginner who is willing to explore the embedded systems programming by doing electronics projects. This book will be helpful for a BeagleBone owner who wants to quickly implement small-scale home automation solutions. Some hands-on experience is expected on C or Python. Some familiarity with electronics is helpful. However, it is not essential.

Conventions

In this book, you will find a number of text styles that distinguish between different kinds of information. Here are some examples of these styles and an explanation of their meaning.

Code words in text, database table names, folder names, filenames, file extensions, pathnames, dummy URLs, user input, and Twitter handles are shown as follows: "It can be turned on by doing shell access to BeagleBone and executing command `sudo ifconfig usb0 up`."

A block of code is set as follows:

```
var b = require('bonescript');
var state = b.HIGH;

b.pinMode("USR3", b.OUTPUT);
b.digitalWrite("USR3", state);

setInterval(blink,1000);

function blink()
{
  if(state == b.LOW)
    state = b.HIGH;
  else
    state = b.LOW;
  b.digitalWrite("USR3", state);
}
```

Any command-line input or output is written as follows:

```
sudo dd  if=<image_file_path> of=/dev/sdx bs=1M ; sync
```

New terms and **important words** are shown in bold. Words that you see on the screen, for example, in menus or dialog boxes, appear in the text like this: "You can stop the loop by clicking on the red **Stop** button in Cloud9."

 Warnings or important notes appear in a box like this.

 Tips and tricks appear like this.

Reader feedback

Feedback from our readers is always welcome. Let us know what you think about this book—what you liked or disliked. Reader feedback is important for us as it helps us develop titles that you will really get the most out of.

To send us general feedback, simply e-mail feedback@packtpub.com, and mention the book's title in the subject of your message.

If there is a topic that you have expertise in and you are interested in either writing or contributing to a book, see our author guide at www.packtpub.com/authors.

Customer support

Now that you are the proud owner of a Packt book, we have a number of things to help you to get the most from your purchase.

Downloading the example code

You can download the example code files from your account at http://www.packtpub.com for all the Packt Publishing books you have purchased. If you purchased this book elsewhere, you can visit http://www.packtpub.com/support and register to have the files e-mailed directly to you.

Downloading the color images of this book

We also provide you with a PDF file that has color images of the screenshots/diagrams used in this book. The color images will help you better understand the changes in the output. You can download this file from: https://www.packtpub.com/sites/default/files/downloads/ProgrammingTheBeagleBone_Graphics.pdf.

Errata

Although we have taken every care to ensure the accuracy of our content, mistakes do happen. If you find a mistake in one of our books—maybe a mistake in the text or the code—we would be grateful if you could report this to us. By doing so, you can save other readers from frustration and help us improve subsequent versions of this book. If you find any errata, please report them by visiting http://www.packtpub.com/submit-errata, selecting your book, clicking on the **Errata Submission Form** link, and entering the details of your errata. Once your errata are verified, your submission will be accepted and the errata will be uploaded to our website or added to any list of existing errata under the Errata section of that title.

To view the previously submitted errata, go to https://www.packtpub.com/books/content/support and enter the name of the book in the search field. The required information will appear under the **Errata** section.

Piracy

Piracy of copyrighted material on the Internet is an ongoing problem across all media. At Packt, we take the protection of our copyright and licenses very seriously. If you come across any illegal copies of our works in any form on the Internet, please provide us with the location address or website name immediately so that we can pursue a remedy.

Please contact us at copyright@packtpub.com with a link to the suspected pirated material.

We appreciate your help in protecting our authors and our ability to bring you valuable content.

Questions

If you have a problem with any aspect of this book, you can contact us at questions@packtpub.com, and we will do our best to address the problem.

1
Cloud9 IDE

BeagleBoard foundation has created a few low power ARM-based open hardware boards. The most successful board among them was BeagleBone Black. Actually, it is a series of boards that match physical size with the same processor and slightly different hardware. There are three variants in this series—BeagleBone White, BeagleBone Black and BeagleBone Green. This book is about programming boards in this BeagleBone series. We will see details about BeagleBone hardware as the first topic of this chapter. Then we will learn how to connect and set up BeagleBone for our work. All BeagleBones come with a programming interface called **BoneScript**. It is a faster and easier way to deal with components of BeagleBone. We are going to use BoneScript for programming in the first part of this book. At the end of this chapter, we will learn about IDE (Integrated Development Environment), which helps us to do programming in BoneScript—Cloud9.

Here are the topics that will be covered in this chapter:

- BeagleBone hardware
- Installing the Debian image on SD card
- Setting up BeagleBone
- bone101 page
- Cloud9
- `Hello World` program

BeagleBone hardware

The BeagleBoard foundation is a non-profit corporation promoting open source hardware and software. It has been releasing low power, hacker-friendly embedded boards since 2008. They have created a few powerful and educational single board computers. These boards are sold to the public under the Creative Commons share-alike license that encourages sharing. These boards are collectively called BeagleBoards. They have a GitHub page at https://github.com/beagleboard. Here you can find hardware information files and software related to released boards. Support for these boards comes from a very active developer community. The BeagleBoard group on Google has more than 10,000 members. You can view posts and join the group here: http://beagleboard.org/Community/Forums. Their IRC (Internet Relay Chat) channel #beagle on freenode is active. You can join the channel and ask questions at http://beagleboard.org/chat. There are more than 500 different projects registered with BeagleBoard at http://beagleboard.org/project.

There are two different series of released boards by beagleboard.org. First is the **BeagleBoard series**. This series has candidates—original BeagleBoard, BeagleBoard-xM and BeagleBoard-X15. These are comparatively big, square-sized boards. Their processors are slightly better in terms of performance and have an additional DSP (Digital Signal Processor) that can do better audio/video processing. These boards have many peripherals available onboard. They are more powerful and comparatively costly. These boards are perfect in scenarios where major audio/video processing is involved or performance is important.

Another series is called the **BeagleBone series**. This series has candidates— BeagleBone White, BeagleBone Black, BeagleBone Green. These boards are compact, lightweight and share the same physical size (3.4 inch × 2.1 inch). They all have the same Texas Instruments AM335x sitara ARM Cortex-A8 processor. These boards lack DSP and lag behind in scenarios with major audio/video processing. But these processors are fine in other scenarios. They come with fewer peripherals on board. You can attach many peripherals externally. They are far cheaper than boards in the BeagleBoard series. They provide many expansion i/o pins of type GPIO/I2C/ SPI/PWM/UART/CAN/ADC. So you can connect lots of sensors, modules, electronic components, displays, and so on. to these boards. All these boards share the same expansion pins layout. This means if you study expansion of one board in the series, the knowledge applies to other boards in the series too. There are small differences in these boards. Please refer to the following table to learn the differences. All these characteristics make BeagleBone a popular choice among hardware hackers. Besides hardware, they can all boot up from the same firmware image. So all software stack is the same for them. These boards can be programmed using the same programming interface. All these boards come with preinstalled Cloud9 IDE, which allows you to write and deploy applications on that board in many programming languages remotely via web browser.

This book covers programming all boards in the BeagleBone series:

	BeagleBone White	BeagleBone Black	BeagleBone Green
Processor	720MHzARM CortexA8	1GHz ARMCortex-A8	1GHz ARMCortex-A8
RAM	256MB DDR2	512MB DDR3	512MB DDR3
Storage	microSD slot only	2/4GB emmc, microSD slot	4GB emmc, microSD slot
Display/ Audio	possible via external cape or USB port	onboard micoHDMI	possible via external cape or USB port
Power connector	via MiniUSB or 5.5mm DC jack(5V)	via MiniUSB or 5.5mm DC jack(5V)	Micro USB only
Boot debugging	onboard serial and JTAG via MiniUSB	via external USB-serial to header pins	via external USB-serial to header pins
Other connector	one standard 2.0 USB host port, one MiniUSB client port, one Ethernet port	One standard 2.0 USBhost port, one MiniUSB client port, one Ethernet port	one UART and one I2C grove connector, one standard 2.0 USB host, one Micro USB client port, one Ethernet port
Expansion	2x 46pin i/o expansion header	2x 46pin i/o expansion header	2x 46pin i/o expansion header

Comparison between different BeagleBones

BeagleBone White (BBW)

This is the first board released in the BeagleBone series. It was released at the end of 2011. At that time, it was just called BeagleBone. Now after more boards have been released in this series, it is called Original BeagleBone or BeagleBone White (BBW). BBW brought single cable development environment. One MiniUSB cable from PC to BBW gives power to BBW, access to storage of BBW and network-over-USB capabilities for communication. The same cable also gives serial access and JTAG access for debugging via FTDI chip. For more information about BeagleBone White, visit the following links:

- http://beagleboard.org/bone
- http://elinux.org/Beagleboard:BeagleBone

The BeagleBone Black board is shown in the following image:

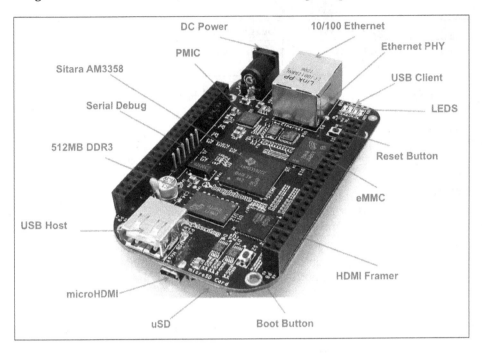

BeagleBone Black (BBB)

BeagleBone Black was released in April 2013. It arrived with more processor speed, more RAM, onboard storage and Micro HDMI connectivity for a lesser price than BBW. BeagleBone Black was very cost-effective and became a huge success. It ranked second consecutively for 2014 and 2015 in a survey of the most popular single board computers conducted by Linux gizmos. BeagleBone Black does not have JTAG access via USB like BBW. You can get serial access via a USB port by help of USB-serial driver in BeagleBone Black only after the board boots. It has a serial pins header. A special USB-serial cable is needed to get serial access via this header to get boot time serial access. Like BBW, single MiniUSB cable from the PC is sufficient to give power to BBB, access to storage of BBB and network-over-USB capabilities for communication. For more information about BeagleBone Black, visit the following links:

- `http://beagleboard.org/black`
- `http://www.elinux.org/Beagleboard:BeagleBoneBlack`

BeagleBone Green (BBG)

Because BeagleBone is an open-source hardware design, anyone can modify design and create a BeagleBone clone (similar to Arduino). BeagleBone Green is a modified version of BeagleBone Black released in October 2015 by SeeedStudio. BeagleBone Green is even cheaper than BeagleBone Black. They removed the Micro HDMI and DC barrel jack. They replaced MiniUSB port with a more common Micro USB port. Internally they are just the same. Two grove connectors are included, which makes it easier to connect a large family of grove sensors and grove modules. For more information about BeagleBone Green, visit the following links:

- http://www.beagleboard.org/green
- http://www.seeedstudio.com/wiki/Beaglebone_green

 It is important to note that throughout this book we will use the word BeagleBone to represent any board (BBW or BBB or BBG) in the BeagleBone series. So BeagleBone setup steps in the book should work for BeagleBone White as well as BeagleBone Black as well as BeagleBone Green.

Installing Debian image on SD card

Now that we know about our hardware, let's install OS. BeagleBone Black and BeagleBone Green come preinstalled with Debian Linux on emmc storage. BeagleBone also supports booting from OS on an SD card. We can use a Linux setup on emmc for exercises in this book. But it is always better to install OS on SD card and boot from it. In case of wrong configuration or unexpected problems, we can install Debian image and start hacking again. Also, it is easier to copy-paste files on an SD card to and from a PC.

The BeagleBone wiki page has a list of OS known to be working on BeagleBone: http://elinux.org/BeagleBone_Operating_Systems. It includes Android, Ubuntu, Angstrom, Minix, WinCE, and so on. Officially Linux distribution **Debian** is supported. All exercises in this book are tested on a wheezy 7.9 Debian image provided by beagleboard.org. Still there should be no problem running these exercises on other Debian versions. Debian is a popular Linux distribution in the embedded world. It is one of the oldest and largest Linux distributions. There are more than 100 Linux distributions derived from Debian. Debian's *stable* branch is known to be one of the best-tested and most bug-free distribution. There are many cases of machines that run for over a year without rebooting. This is important for unattended embedded systems. Debian has thousands of installable packages. It uses **APT (Advanced Package Tool)** using deb packages. You can get more information about Debian on http://debian.org.

When you connect the BeagleBone to PC using a USB-to-MiniUSB cable (Micro USB for BeagleBone Green), it gets detected as flash drive providing you with a local copy of the documentation and drivers. When it autoruns, you see the browser opened with the page **Getting Started**. If it does not run automatically, you can manually open the file START.htm or the README.htm file inside the BeagleBone flash drive. This HTML page has a link to "update to latest software" on the left. It provides you with a step-by-step procedure with screenshots to install the latest prebuilt Debian image on the SD card. An online version of this webpage is available at: http://beagleboard.org/getting-started#update.

Here are the important steps to install the latest Debian image on the BeagleBone:

1. Latest supported images of all BeagleBoards are available at http://beagleboard.org/latest-images. Download a Debian image for BeagleBone on your PC. The same image works on BeagleBone White, Black and Green.

2. These images come compressed. On a Linux system you can extract it by right-clicking to that file in File Manager and choosing **Extract Here**. On a Windows system, you can extract it using decompression software 7zip available at http://www.7-zip.org/download.html.You will get an .img file. This is an actual image file.

3. Now, attach a USB SD card reader to your PC. On a Linux system, you can dump an .img file on a SD card using the following command. You need to find the name of the SD card file. You can get that in dmesg command output after you connect the SD card. Put that in place of sdx in command.

    ```
    sudo dd  if=<image_file_path> of=/dev/sdx bs=1M ; sync
    ```

    On a Windows system, you can use image writer software like win32diskimager, available at: http://sourceforge.net/projects/win32diskimager/files/latest/download. Select .img file and correct the SD card drive and click the **write** button to dump an image on the SD card.

     Warning: Be careful when selecting and formatting SD card files/drives. The wrong selection for an SD card can damage data on other storage.

4. Push this SD card in the BeagleBone SD card holder. Give power supply to the board and you should see user LEDs blinking, which is sign of life. In case you want to make sure you are booting from the SD card and not emmc, get shell access (covered in the next topic) and edit files /etc/issue and /etc/issue.net on the SD card to print that it is booted from the SD card. The next the shell access login will show that message.

Setting up BeagleBone

Embedded boards lack rich programming environment like x86 Desktop PC. Often they are connected to x86 Desktop for programming. Before starting programming, we need to connect BeagleBone to PC and set up the working environment. Let us see different ways to connect to BeagleBone and how to start Cloud9 programming IDE and the useful bone101 page. If you connect the BeagleBone via any one the following ways successfully, you can skip others. You will need a little Linux commands knowledge here. If any of these connection steps do not work, try the steps given in Troubleshooting section. The most common problem is the power supply. USB 2.0 is designed to supply max 500mA current, which is fine if you are not attaching peripherals to BeagleBone. But if you are connecting Ethernet, HDMI or USB devices, you should use a 5V 2A power adapter with 5.5mm DC barrel jack to power up BeagleBone. You can get it at https://www.sparkfun.com/products/12889. On BeagleBone Green, you will have to use a 5V 2A Micro USB power adapter. You can get it at: https://www.sparkfun.com/products/12890.

By default, you can login as username debian and password temppwd on default Debian images for BeagleBone. This user has sudo access to all the commands in the current Debian image. The board has to be secured before starting to use it. Once logged in, you should change the password of debian user using the command passwd. You can also login as root with no password when asked. You should login as a root user and change the root password too using the same command.

Direct connection to monitor and keyboard

BeagleBone Black comes with a Micro HDMI port. You can connect it to HDMI monitor/TV/display using Micro HDMI-HDMI cable. You can attach USB keyboard and mouse to USB port directly or using USB hub. There is no need of a host laptop/desktop PC for this connectivity. After GUI login, you can get shell access by opening terminal emulator like lxterminal. You can browse local files on BeagleBone. You can open the browser and visit http://beaglebone.local to see the bone101 page and http://beaglebone.local:3000 to open Cloud9 IDE. There are HDMI/DVI/VGA/LCD add-on cape boards that fit on the BeagleBone and help you to achieve similar connectivity.

Ethernet over USB

For this connection, you need to connect the BeagleBone to the host laptop/desktop PC using a USB to MiniUSB cable (Micro USB in case of BeagleBone Green). This is a popular way of accessing BeagleBone and programming on Cloud9 IDE. BeagleBone treats its MiniUSB port as a virtual Ethernet port using a special driver. With the help of this driver, one can attach an IP address to MiniUSB port and access it like the Ethernet. By default, it has the static address 192.168.7.2. In order to communicate with it, you need to have usbnet/RNDIS driver installed on a connected PC. It comes preinstalled in most of the Linux systems. In that case, you will get a new Ethernet entry in output of command ifconfig. On a Windows system, you need to install RNDIS drivers manually. BeagleBone has a RNDIS driver installable in its fat storage. Please refer to the *Installing Debian image on SD card* section, to open the Getting Started webpage. This page has a local link to an executable file that installs RNDIS and other drivers. Click on the correct driver link on the Getting Started page according to your PC OS. You can also install the driver manually from the Drivers folder in BeagleBone's fat storage.

After installing the RNDIS2 driver, you will see the new network card interface in network settings. It should get IP address 192.168.7.1 via dhcp. If not, manually give the IP address to new network interface on your PC – 192.168.7.1. You can open the bone101 page by putting http://192.168.7.2 in the browser address bar and Cloud9 IDE with http://192.168.7.2:3000/. You can get shell access on BeagleBone by running command ssh root@192.168.7.2 in the Linux/Mac terminal. On Windows systems, you will need terminal emulator like putty for this. You need to connect BeagleBone to the router via an Ethernet or USB-Wi-Fi in order to get Internet access. You can use a VNC connection to get BeagleBone GUI access. It is covered in a later section.

Troubleshooting

- Use Firefox/Chrome only for connection. Internet Explorer is not supported.
- Sometimes, BeagleBone's usb0 (Ethernet over USB) interface does not get turned on automatically. It can be turned on by doing shell access to BeagleBone and executing the command:

  sudo ifconfig usb0 up.

- Refer to the table at end of this topic to learn different ways you can get shell access. After getting shell access to BeagleBone, you can use utilities like ifconfig, ping and dmesg to debug further.

- If you were not able to install the RNDIS driver from the BeagleBone flash storage, you can install drivers from http://beagleboard.org/static/Drivers.

Ethernet port or USB Wi-Fi adapter

BeagleBone comes with an Ethernet port. You can connect a laptop/desktop PC and BeagleBone via a Ethernet cable directly or preferably via a router. By default, the Ethernet port of BeagleBone is configured to get automatic IP address via dhcp. There should be a dhcp server configured in your network to get the IP address assigned to the BeagleBone Ethernet port. Ethernet port connection with the Internet-connected router gives your BeagleBone access to the Internet. Then you can install/upgrade packages on the Internet. Many programs in this book rely on Internet connection to the BeagleBone. This is the most preferred way of connection as far as this book is concerned.

Another option is to connect the USB Wi-Fi adapter to BeagleBone and then connect your PC to BeagleBone via its IP address. You need to install the correct kernel firmware package according to your Wi-Fi adapter chipset using the command `apt-get`. Once configured, this connection works the same as the Ethernet connection.

If you connect it via Ethernet or a USB-Wi-Fi adapter, you can browse `http://<<Beaglebone's ip address>>` for the bone101 page and `http://<<Beaglebone's ip address>>:3000` for Cloud9 IDE. BeagleBone Ethernet gets its IP address via DHCP. You can find out the IP address of BeagleBone from the router web login. You can also get shell access and run the command *ifconfig* to find out the IP address of the BeagleBone. Different methods to get BeagleBone shell access are given in the table at the end of this topic. So, if the BeagleBone IP address is found to be `192.168.1.2`, then the bone101 page will be accessible at `http://192.168.1.2`. You can also `ssh` to `root@<<Beaglebone's ip address>>` to get shell access via Ethernet. You can do VNC connection to get BeagleBone GUI access, which is covered in the next section.

Troubleshooting

* Troubleshooting Ethernet/USB-Wi-Fi steps follows the same steps as Ethernet over USB troubleshooting. But for the Ethernet port, the IP addressing scheme will be different than `192.168.7.x`.

* In case of a problem with a USB-Wi-Fi adapter, make a serial or Ethernet over USB connection to BeagleBone to get shell access and check whether it is getting detected by the command `dmesg`. If it is detected correctly, you can configure it using `iwconfig` and `ifconfig`.

VNC

You can also connect via **VNC (Virtual Network Computing)**. It is a remote desktop connection. You need to connect via the Ethernet over USB or Ethernet or USB-Wi-Fi method first to do a VNC connection. Debian for BeagleBone comes with tightvncserver preinstalled. To set up VNC get shell access to BeagleBone and run the command vncserver on it as a Debian user. Download VNC client software on PC and connect to server beaglebone:1. You will get a similar GUI like you get on an HDMI connection. You will be able to get shell access via the lxterminal terminal emulator, browse the bone101 page at http://beaglebone.local and browse cloud9 IDE at http://beaglebone.local:3000. As BeagleBone White and BeagleBone Green do not have an HDMI port, this option is useful if you want GUI access.

Troubleshooting

- The vncserver display does not always run on :1. Command vncserver prints the name of the display it is running on. Note it down and use it when connecting from the VNC viewer.

- Sometimes the IP address works instead of the name. Specify<beaglebone ip address>:1 as the server display.

- The VNC session might not use the lxde window manager. Currently Debian uses openbox window manager for the VNC session of the debian user. It shows the desktop with no icon or panel. You get shell and browser access by right-clicking on the desktop.

Serial Connection

Serial connection gives you a booting log and then a SSH-like command line interface. Please note that you cannot access Cloud9 or bone101 page or GUI using serial connection. BeagleBone provides two types of serial access. One is using a pseudo USB-serial driver on a USB port. You get a SSH-like shell access by this method. As a USB-serial driver starts working after kernel booting, you do not get boot logs by this method. BeagleBone Black on MiniUSB port and BeagleBone Green on Micro USB port provide this type of serial access. When you connect by these methods, BeagleBone appears as serial device on the connected PC. On Windows, it appears as serial COM port in the device manager. Note down the COM port number in the device manager and connect to that port via putty or hyperterminal specifying baud rate 115200.

On the Linux system, check kernel messages of the PC using the command `dmesg` to find out the name of the device it got detected as. It gets detected as `/dev/ttyUSB0` by default. You can use this command to connect it serially:

```
sudo screen /dev/ttyUSB0 115200
```

When you are done, press *Ctrl + A* then *K* to exit the screen.

Another type of serial connection possible on BeagleBone is via using a hardware chip that is responsible for making a serial connection. As an external chip is doing the work, this method gives boot time logs as well as shell access when booting is done. This connection is the only way to get logs when BeagleBone is failing to boot properly. It is useful to configure Ethernet, and debug problems. BeagleBone White has FTDI USB-to-serial conversion chip onboard. It gives serial access over a MiniUSB port. For BeagleBone Black and BeagleBone Green, the onboard USB-serial chip is absent. But there are serial header pins available onboard. You need a special USB-serial TTL cable to attach to these header pins. Any FTDI or PL2303 or cp210x chip based USB TTL cable can be used here. The FTDI cable from Adafruit is popular which can be found at `https://www.adafruit.com/products/70`. You will have to install drivers corresponding to the chip used in the cable. Drivers for these chips come preinstalled in most of the Linux systems and the serial port gets detected as `/dev/ttUSB0` by default. You can connect using the `screen` command we covered in previous paragraph. Windows drivers for FTDI or PL2303 of CP210x are available on vendor websites. Once you install the driver, you will be able to locate the COM port in the device manager and connect via the hyperterminal or putty:

	Physical ports	**GUI**	**Shell**	**bone101**	**Cloud9**	**Internet**
Direct monitor and keyboard connection	HDMI & regular USB port	Yes	Yes	Yes	Yes	Possible via Ethernet or USB-Wi-Fi
Ethernet over USB	Mini/Micro USB	via VNC	via SSH	Yes	Yes	Possible via Ethernet or USB-Wi-Fi
Ethernet or USB-Wi-Fi	Ethernet or regular USB port	via VNC	via SSH	Yes	Yes	Yes if connected to router with the Internet
VNC	Mini/Micro USB or Ethernet	Yes	Yes	Yes	Yes	Possible via Ethernet or USB-Wi-Fi
Serial connection	Mini/Micro USB or serial-header	___	Yes	___	___	Possible via Ethernet or USB-Wi-Fi

Besides all these options, Cloud9 IDE has one tab inside it, which gives you a root shell. So, if you have Cloud9 access, there is no need to connect via terminal emulator or SSH to get BeagleBone shell access. Here is a helpful link on BeagleBone wiki about connecting BeagleBone `http://elinux.org/Beagleboard:Terminal_Shells`.

The bone101 page

We have seen several ways to connect to BeagleBone and access the bone101 webpage. This web page can be accessed on web server running on port 80 on Beagelbone. This page has information about the board and some examples of BoneScript code:

The top-most green frame tells you that the board is connected. If your board is not connected, this frame will be of orange color and it will ask you to enter the IP address of the board. The left side pane has links to supported BoneScript and JavaScript functions. The remaining page gives miscellaneous information including available OS, upgrading OS, Cloud9 quickstart information, and expansion I/O pin details.

You can always get help about BoneScript library functions from the left frame on the bone101 page. These function help information have example code snippets. These code snippets come with a **run** and **restore** button. If your board is showing a green frame indicating that you are connected, then you can run these examples directly from the bone101 page. You can modify the code on the webpage and run new code by pressing the **run** button. If you want to go back to the unmodified original example code, press the **restore** button. You can even open this page from a smartphone browser with the correct BeagleBone IP address and run code from there.

If you are connected to BeagleBone via Ethernet over USB, you get connected to the topmost green frame automatically. If you are connected to the Ethernet port, you will see an orange frame asking for the IP address. You can get the IP address of the Ethernet port from your router weblogin or by getting shell access and running `ifconfig`. You can enter that IP and you will get green frame saying **You are connected**. Then you can explore online help and execute the example code.

A later part in the webpage gives a step-by-step procedure with screenshots to start Cloud9 IDE and run the first BoneScript program. The last part of this page gives details about BeagleBone Black hardware. It has links to the online hardware design files and wiki page. This section gives pin details of expansion headers like which pins have `GPIO`, analog input, `PWM`, `UART`, `I2C` and `SPI` capabilities. We will need this information throughout the book. To get updated help information and examples of BoneScript, visit `http://beagleboard.org/Support/BoneScript/`. This page allows us to connect BeagleBone and run BoneScript example code on BeagleBone similar to the bone101 page.

Cloud9 IDE

Cloud9 IDE runs on port number `3000` on BeagleBone. The *Setting up BeagleBone* section covered many ways to connect to BeagleBone and open Cloud9 IDE. After connecting to BeagleBone and opening Cloud9 via any one of these ways, we are ready to explore BeagleBone's default programming IDE.

Cloud9 is a web-based IDE to develop primarily JavaScript and Node.js applications. It also supports many other programming languages including PHP, Java, Python and Ruby. Cloud9 runs on the web which means it works inside a browser. There is no difference if you are using Windows, Linux or MAC OS on your PC or even from your smartphone. If you are using a supported Firefox or Chrome browser on a remote PC/smartphone, you can run Cloud9 and do programming on BeagleBone. Cloud9 allows many developers to code simultaneously on single project through the web. It supports instant deployment to many well-known cloud platforms like Microsoft Azure, Google App Engine and OpenShift. It is open source software and maintained by a company called Cloud9 IDE, Inc. You can get the source code here: `https://github.com/c9/core`:

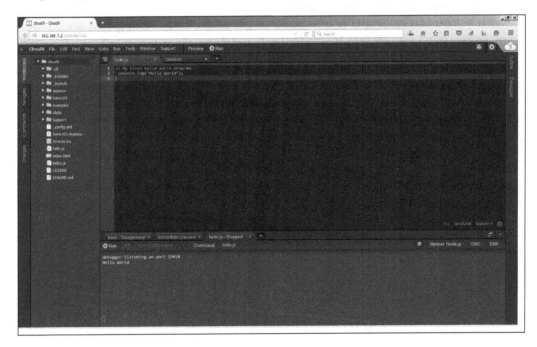

Cloud9 is made up of multiple child windows inside. In the leftmost windows you can select a project related window among **Workspace** or **Navigate** or **Commands**. The **Workspace** window has a tree view that expands and collapses project files. You can add new, rename and delete project files from this window. At the bottom, there is a console window to display program output, compilation errors, and `console.log()` messages. When you run any program, you get output printed in this window. You can add a new JavaScript immediate tab in this window. It is useful to evaluate expressions, execute statements and print variables values. You can also add a `bash shell` in this window tab. You can run commands directly on BeagleBone from here. At the right, there is a place for toolbars. **Debugger** and **Outline** toolbars take place in this area. Expand the **debugger** toolbar when you want to debug a program line by line. The middle empty part is the code editor area. Here actual code gets written. It has very small pane area at the left side. It shows line numbers and breakpoints, errors, and warning signs corresponding to that line. Cloud9 supports multiple tabs to edit many files simultaneously. It provides code completion features for snippets and identifiers. It has rich debugging features like setting breakpoints and step into/step over. It provides dragging and dropping of files from computer to code area. This way, you can add new ready-made code to your project. There are many customization options available with a menu bar at the uppermost side.

We are going to use Cloud9 for all BoneScript programs. There are some ready-made files with code in the demo directory. But they need some hardware setup. So, we will skip them. The best way to get help is to visit the bone101 page or `http://beagleboard.org/Support/BoneScript/`.

Hello World program

Let's do a quick and dirty `Hello World` JavaScript program. In this program, we are just printing `Hello World` in the console view provided by Cloud9:

1. Go to the **File** menu. Click on the **New File** button. You will see a new code editor tab opened with title `Untitled1`.

2. Write the following code in the code editor view:

```
// My first hello world program.
 console.log("Hello World");
```

Downloading the example code

You can download the example code files from your account at `http://www.packtpub.com` for all the Packt Publishing books you have purchased. If you purchased this book elsewhere, you can visit `http://www.packtpub.com/support` and register to have the files e-mailed directly to you.

3. Go to the **File** menu again and save as `hello.js`. Now, you should see the tab title is changed from `Untitled1` to `hello.js`. Now Cloud9 knows this is JavaScript program. It will highlight the program with different colors.

4. Click on the **run** button at the top of screen. You will see the **Debugger** toolbar from right side is expanded to the **Debug** pane. Click on the **Resume** button on expanded pane or press the *F8* key. You should see the `Hello World` text in the output view at the bottom.

Explanation

In this tiny code, the first line is the comment. JavaScript supports C and C++ style commenting. So the pattern `/* ... */` is used in multi-line commenting and the pattern `//` is used for single line commenting. The second line is calling the `log()` method on the object `console`. We have given the string `Hello World` as a parameter to the `log()` method. A semicolon `;` denotes a terminated statement. Here, the `console` object provides access to the browser's debugging console. `console.log()` is a method to print string. It prints `Hello World` in the console.

As we are using a built-in JavaScript object, we have not loaded a JavaScript module/library. You can try more methods provided by the console object. You can get a detailed document about JavaScript at: `http://www.w3schools.com/js/` and `https://developer.mozilla.org/en-US/docs/Web/JavaScript`.

Summary

This chapter covered all the prerequisites to get programming IDE access on BeagleBone with the latest software. In this chapter we learned about different boards available in the BeagleBone series and their hardware differences. Then we learned how to install the latest Debian image on BeagleBone and various ways to connect to BeagleBone with troubleshooting steps. Once connected, we can visit the bone101 HTML page, which has lots of information about BeagleBone. It also provides help pages for JavaScript and BoneScript functions. Then we started using Cloud9 IDE. It is a web-based IDE that runs on port number `3000` on BeagleBone. In the end, we created our first JavaScript program that prints `Hello World`.

Now, we are ready with IDE and we know how to compile and run a program on BeagleBone. In the next chapters, we will write programs that interact with the physical environment.

2
Blinking Onboard LEDs

In the previous chapter, we learned about the Cloud9 IDE that comes preinstalled on the BeagleBone standard Debian distribution. It also comes with the preinstalled BoneScript library. This library provides you functions to communicate with various electronic components that can be connected to BeagleBone. These components can be LEDs, buttons, buzzers, various sensors, motors, and others. Connecting external components to BeagleBone needs some manual work such as attaching jumper wires, soldering, or using breadboard. This can be tedious for a new user. Fortunately, BeagleBone comes with four onboard LEDs. We can directly program them without doing any manual connection. In this chapter, we will blink onboard LEDs by our program using BoneScript functions.

The following topics will be covered in this chapter:

- Digital I/O
- Digital I/O functions – `pinMode()` and `digitalWrite()`
- Program to turn onboard LED ON and OFF
- Quick program to blink onboard LED
- Make our program better
- Dancing LEDs
- Dancing LEDs in both directions

Digital I/O

In real life, there are many things that can have only two possible states, for example, a book is either open or closed, your smartphone screen can be locked or unlocked, power switches at home can be on or off. This holds true for some input and output components attached to BeagleBone as well. For example, LEDs can be either **on** or **off**, a push button can be in a **pushed** state or **normal** state (often referred to as a **closed** or **open** state). These components with only two possible states are **digital components**.

If you look at the nearby area of the BeagleBone processor AM335X chip carefully, you will see that many physical lines are connecting the processor to various other chips or components on the board. Each of these lines connects to the processor at a point called **Ball** or **Pin**. The BeagleBone processor has several such pins to communicate with outside chips and components. Among these pins, some pins are dedicated to deal with digital components only. We cannot attach analog components to these pins. These pins are called **digital I/O pins**. You can write either a HIGH or LOW state on the digital output pin through software. When you write HIGH, the pin gets positive voltage, and when you write LOW, the pin gets zero voltage from the processor. You can read the state of digital input pins as HIGH or LOW according to the voltage set by the component connected to this pin. Onboard LEDs and buttons of BeagleBone are connected to digital I/O pins of the processor. So if we write a HIGH state on the digital output pin connected to an onboard LED, that LED will glow.

Digital electronics works at two logic levels—HIGH (Binary 1) or LOW (Binary 0). Different boards follow different voltage ranges to represent HIGH and LOW. BeagleBone works on a 3.3 voltage level. If we program a digital pin as HIGH on BeagleBone, 3.3 volts is set on this pin. So, whatever digital component is attached to this pin, say, an LED, gets 3.3 volts and the current flows through it turning it on. As a programmer, you need not know about the voltage and current flowing from digital components if they are compatible with the 3.3V logic. Let's see the functions that we will use in our LED blinking program.

Digital I/O functions - pinMode() and digitalWrite()

Digital components can be of an input or output type. A push button is an input type digital component. It does not make sense to write on a push button. LEDs and buzzers are output type digital components. We can program a digital I/O pin on BeagleBone to communicate with both the input and output type of components. However, it has to be specified first whether we are going to use that pin as an input or output pin. Once specified, the pin acts in that direction only. We will learn in detail about this in the next chapter. To blink an LED, we need to specify that we are going to use that pin as the output. Then only we can program it to turn on or off.

Debian on BeagleBone comes with a preinstalled Node.js library called **BoneScript**. It provides simple Arduino-like functions to interface the BeagleBone hardware. So, it becomes easier to program in BoneScript if there is prior experience in programming Arduino. The Bone101 page that we studied in the previous chapter has detailed information and many examples on BoneScript APIs. This is an open source library. You can get the source code at `https://github.com/jadonk/bonescript`.

Before doing the actual programming, let's learn essential functions required to communicate with the digital components. BoneScript provides you the `pinMode()` function to set the direction of the specified pin. The direction can be the input or output. Once the direction is set, the pin will work in that direction only. If you want to change the direction, you need to use the `pinMode()` function again. Here is a prototype of the `pinMode()` function:

```
pinMode(pin, direction)
```

Where

`pin` – BeagleBone pin identifier string

`direction` – Input or Output direction

The `pinMode()` function takes the name of the pin to be selected as the first argument. The second argument indicates if it is connected to the Input or Output type component. Once the Output type is specified, we can make the pin high or low. This is achieved by the BoneScript `digitalWrite()` function. Here is a prototype of the `digitalWrite()` function:

```
digitalWrite(pin, value)
```

Where

`pin` – BeagleBone pin identifier string

`value` – HIGH or LOW

This function takes the name of the selected pin as the first argument and the second argument as a HIGH or LOW value. It writes this value on the specified pin. This will be clear when we write a program using these functions. These functions are similar to the pinMode() and digitalWrite() functions from the Arduino world.

 Actually, the pinMode() function takes more than two arguments. However, they are optional and not required for our current goal of blinking LEDs. We will continue studying only required parts to avoid confusion throughout the book.

Program to turn onboard LED ON and OFF

We have collected enough information to program an onboard LED. BeagleBone comes with four small onboard user LEDs. They are located above the mini USB port. They are labeled as USER LEDs and named **USER0**, **USER1**, **USER2**, and **USER3** LEDs. You can refer to the following image. We will turn on USER3 LED, which is configured by default to turn on each time the emmc is accessed:

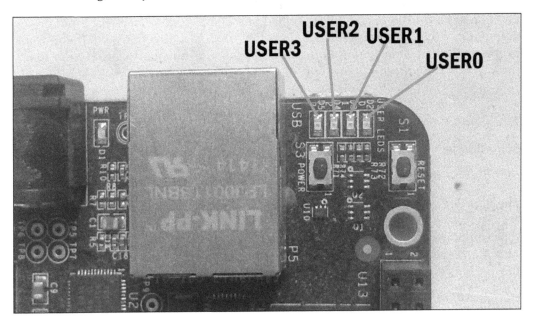

Create a new file in Cloud9 as we did in the previous chapter. Write the following code in it and save it as `turnOnUSER3.js`. Run the program and you should see USER3 LED turned on. The code for `turnOnUSER3.js` is as follows:

```
var b = require('bonescript');
b.pinMode("USR3", b.OUTPUT);
b.digitalWrite("USR3", b.HIGH);
```

Now, turning the USER3 LED off is straightforward. You just need to change `b.HIGH` to `b.LOW` in the `digitalWrite()` function. Save the code as `turnOffUSER3.js`. Run the program and you should see the USER3 LED turned off. The code for `turnOffUSER3.js` is as follows:

```
var b = require('bonescript');
b.pinMode("USR3", b.OUTPUT);
b.digitalWrite("USR3", b.LOW);
```

Program explanation

This code is in **JavaScript**. If you know JavaScript, well and good. Even if you do not know, it should not be a big problem. For our work, we need some JavaScript-specific details. We will cover these when we use them. Here is a line-by-line explanation of the preceding code used to turn onboard LED ON and OFF:

1. We first import the BoneScript library and assign it to the b variable. Now, b is the handle for the BoneScript library. We will get all the BoneScript functionality by `b.<function name>` and variables by `b.<variable name>`. The BoneScript library provides several functions that are useful to interact with BeagleBone.

2. We are declaring here that the USER3 pin will be used as the output. We set the direction as output. This means it is possible to only write on it and not read from it.

3. Set USER3 LED's pin to HIGH or LOW. The `digitalWrite()` function in BoneScript is settings USER3 to HIGH or LOW. If set to HIGH, the LED glows. If set to LOW, the LED gets turned off. In the BoneScript code, HIGH is set to 1 and LOW is set to 0. So, you can also use the value 1 instead of HIGH and 0 instead of LOW.

Note that we wrote USR3 in the program and not USER3. BoneScript refers to it as USR3 in its code.

Note that function names are made up of two words. The first word is written in lowercase. The first character of the second word is in uppercase and all the remaining characters are in lowercase. This type of notation is called camel case. This increases the readability of code. It is used to name functions as well as variables. Camel case notation logic is not limited to two words. You can have a multiword function name that follows this notation. JavaScript prefers the camel case notation.

We turned the LED on/off with our program. This type of showing the physical output is different from the usual way of showing the GUI/CLI output. This type of programming is called **physical computing**. It involves sensing/getting data from the environment (physical world) and responding to it interactively using physical output components such as LED, buzzer, relay, motor, and so on. Physical computing is used heavily in embedded systems.

Quick program to blink onboard LED

Now that we have written a program to turn the USER3 LED on and off, let's write a program to blink this LED. Type the following program in Cloud9, save it as blinkOnboardLED.js, and run it. Your USER3 LED should start blinking each second. This is an infinite loop. You can stop the loop by clicking on the red **Stop** button in Cloud9. The code for blinkOnboardLED.js is as follows:

```
var b = require('bonescript');
var state = b.HIGH;

b.pinMode("USR3", b.OUTPUT);
b.digitalWrite("USR3", state);

setInterval(blink,1000);

function blink()
{
  if(state == b.LOW)
    state = b.HIGH;
  else
    state = b.LOW;
  b.digitalWrite("USR3", state);
}
```

Program explanation

We want to blink the LED after each second. If one wants to code this in C, they will undoubtedly use the `sleep()` function in the loop. However, JavaScript is used in web development mostly. It executes client-side code and talks with the web server asynchronously. So, it has different rules. It prefers asynchronous event handler functions over sleeping the whole JavaScript engine. There is no sleep-like function in JavaScript. Instead, it provides timing events. We need to write an event handler function and event condition. The handler function gets called asynchronously when the timing event condition is met. So, the JavaScript execution engine does not have to keep on waiting until the condition is met. It can go ahead executing the next code. These handler functions are callback functions in event-driven programming. This whole concept is the same as registering the signal and writing the signal handler function for that signal.

The following is a line-by-line explanation of the preceding code:

1. We are importing the BoneScript library and assign it to the `b` variable.

2. The new variable is named `state` and assigned a HIGH value. We will assign it to the USER3 LED soon.

3. We declare that the USER3 pin will be used for the output using the `pinMode()` function.

4. Write the `state` variable (which is HIGH) on the USER3 LED. USER3 is turned on at this point.

5. We are creating a timer event, which will be triggered each second. The JavaScript `setInterval()` method provides the functionality to execute a block of code again and again after a specified time. This block of code should be put in the `setInterval()` method. The `setInterval()` method takes the handler function to be called repetitively as the first argument. It takes second argument as interval in milliseconds after which the handler function should be called repeatedly. Here, we are calling the `blink()` function after 1,000 milliseconds (one second) again and again. This is similar to the `loop()` function in the Arduino world.

6. Now, we write the `blink()` function, which will be called after each second. The `blink()` function is the timer event handler function that toggles the USER3 LED on or off. We check the current value of the `state` variable in the `blink()` function. If it is LOW, then `state` is changed to a HIGH value. Otherwise, it is set to a LOW value. Later, we set USER3 to the `state` variable.

> If you noticed, we did not specify a variable type at the time of declaring the variable. In JavaScript, a variable's type is set based on the value it got.

Program execution

When we run this program, it will first set the USER3 LED to HIGH. This results in turning on the V16 (or GPIO1_24) pin of the processor internally, and 3.3 voltage is put across this pin. As the V16 pin is connected to the USER3 LED, the current starts flowing through the USER3 LED and it glows. For more details, check the *User LEDs* section in the *BeagleBone System Reference Manual(SRM),*. This manual PDF file can be found in the FAT partition of BeagleBone. You can get the online version from `https://github.com/CircuitCo/BeagleBone-Black/blob/rev_b/BBB_SRM.pdf`.

Then, the `setInterval()` method will set the timer with the `blink()` callback function for one second. This means that `blink()` will be called automatically after each second. At the first call, as the `state` variable has the HIGH value, it will be changed to LOW and `digitalWrite()` will be called. Control will go in the BoneScript library code and the library will write LOW on the `sysfs` file associated with the USER3 LED. The current will stop flowing through USER3 and it will be turned off.

After one second, the `blink()` function will be called again. This time, the `state` variable has the LOW value. It will be changed to HIGH and the USER3 LED will glow again for a second. The `blink()` function will be called again and the USER3 LED will turn off again, and so on.

Make our program better

If you executed the previous program a few times, you would have noticed that though the program is getting executed correctly, it does not exit by itself. It has an infinite loop of timer. So, it needs to be stopped manually. If the LED state is on at the time of stopping the program, it will remain on later. Let's add a new timer that will trigger after a minute to exit the program and turn off the USER3 LED if it is on. Also, let's change the hard-coded values that we used in the previous program. Type the following program in Cloud9, save it as `blinkOnboardLED2.js`, and run it. The program should stop automatically after a minute with the USER3 LED always off. The code for `blinkOnboardLED2.js` is as follows:

```
var b = require('bonescript');
var led = "USR3";
var loopTime = 1000;
var exitTime = 60000;
var state = b.HIGH;

b.pinMode(led, b.OUTPUT);
```

```
  b.digitalWrite(led, state);

  var loopTimer = setInterval(blink, loopTime);
  setTimeout(exitProgram,exitTime);

  function blink()
  {
    if(state == b.LOW)
      state = b.HIGH;
    else
      state = b.LOW;
    b.digitalWrite(led, state);
  }
  function exitProgram()
  {
    b.digitalWrite(led,b.LOW);
    clearInterval(loopTimer);
  }
```

Program explanation

This code is small addition to the previous LED blinking code:

1. We hard-coded the values of the USER3 LED and blinking time in the last program. Here, we declared them in the beginning and initialized them with appropriate values. Now, just by changing the values of the variables at the beginning of the code, we can test different behaviors easily.

2. This time, we are naming the timer created by setInterval() as loopTimer. It is scheduled to tick after each second. Our program cannot exit if loopTimer is not cleared. The new timer event setTimeout() method asks the system to call the exitProgram() handler function after 60,000 milliseconds (one minute) only once. Unlike setInterval(), the setTimeout() function generates a timer event only once.

3. The `blink()` function is the same as in the earlier program. This function turns the LED on/off after each second. The new `exitProgram()` callback function is added. In `exitProgram()`, the LED is turned off first. Then, the `clearInterval()` method stops further execution of the `blink()` function associated with the `loopTimer` timer event. The `clearInterval()` method takes the timer name as an argument. When `loopTimer` is cleared, there is nothing left for execution and the program exits. Thus, the LED will always be off when the program finishes. The `setTimeout()`, `setInterval()`, and `clearInterval()` methods come from an HTML DOM window object. The HTML DOM window object is a top-level object in the JavaScript hierarchy and it represents the web browser window. If you are curious, you can refer to `http://www.w3schools.com/js/js_timing.asp`.

If you have connected BeagleBone via Ethernet and your smartphone is in the same LAN network, then you can open Cloud9 in your smartphone browser (by opening `<beagleboneip>:3000`) and run the program. In this case, you will be able to start/stop the LED blinking remotely via a smartphone. This hack is applicable to all the programs in this book.

Until now, we have been running the Cloud9 IDE to execute our programs. What if we want to run it directly without Cloud9? Cloud9 IDE uses the `/usr/bin/node` interpreter to execute the code. Can the IDE be bypassed in order to run the BoneScript program directly by the Node interpreter? The answer is yes.

All the files created in the Cloud9 IDE get stored in the `/var/lib/cloud9` directory by default. Get the shell access of BeagleBone in any of the ways suggested in *Chapter 1*, *Cloud9 IDE*, and run the following command:

```
node /var/lib/cloud9/blinkOnboardLED2.js
```

You will see the USER3 LED blinking until a minute. You can create JavaScript programs in your favorite editor and run these programs by changing the filename in the preceding command. This way, we can bypass Cloud9 totally.

Dancing LEDs

BeagleBone has four onboard LEDs adjacent to each other. Let's create an LED on/off pattern so that we get an illusion of dancing LEDs. We will follow the turning on the LED sequence: USER0 -> USER1 -> USER2 -> USER3 -> USER0 -> USER1 -> USER2 -> USER3 -> USER0, and so on. This will give the illusion that light is traveling from USER0 to USER3 in loops. Type the following program in Cloud9, save it as `danceLEDs.js` and run it. The code for `danceLEDs.js` is as follows:

```
var b = require('bonescript');
```

```
var glowTime = 100;
var exitTime = 30000;
var tempTimer;

b.pinMode("USR0", b.OUTPUT);
b.pinMode("USR1", b.OUTPUT);
b.pinMode("USR2", b.OUTPUT);
b.pinMode("USR3", b.OUTPUT);

var exitTimer = setTimeout(exitProgram,exitTime);
glowUser0();

function glowUser0()
{
  b.digitalWrite("USR3", b.LOW);
  b.digitalWrite("USR0", b.HIGH);
  tempTimer = setTimeout(glowUser1,glowTime);
}

function glowUser1()
{
  b.digitalWrite("USR0", b.LOW);
  b.digitalWrite("USR1", b.HIGH);
  tempTimer = setTimeout(glowUser2,glowTime);
}

function glowUser2()
{
  b.digitalWrite("USR1", b.LOW);
  b.digitalWrite("USR2", b.HIGH);
  tempTimer = setTimeout(glowUser3,glowTime);
}

function glowUser3()
{
  b.digitalWrite("USR2", b.LOW);
  b.digitalWrite("USR3", b.HIGH);
  tempTimer = setTimeout(glowUser0,glowTime);
}

function exitProgram()
{
  b.digitalWrite("USR0",b.LOW);
```

```
    b.digitalWrite("USR1",b.LOW);
    b.digitalWrite("USR2",b.LOW);
    b.digitalWrite("USR3",b.LOW);
    clearTimeout(tempTimer);
}
```

Program explanation

Though this program looks bigger, it has lots of repetitive code. All the functions except `exitProgram()` are almost identical. The `glowTime` and `exitTime` variables are soft-coded. Set them to different values and observe the difference.

The following is a line-by-line explanation:

1. First, we mark all the LEDs as the output.

2. Create a timer event named `exitTimer` with `setTimeout()`. It will clear the `tempTimer` event and exit the program after 30 seconds.

3. The `glowUser0()` function turns on the USER0 LED and calls the `glowUser1()` function with a delay of `glowTime` (100 milliseconds). As this is `setTimeout()`, the calling of `glowUser1()` will be only once.

4. The `glowUser1()` function turns off the USER0 LED that was just turned on in the previous step. Then, it will turn on the USER1 LED and call `glowUser2()` only once with a delay of 100 milliseconds.

5. The `glowUser2()` function turns off USER1 that we turned on earlier. Then, it will turn on the USER2 LED and call `glowUser3()` only once with a delay of 100 milliseconds.

6. The `glowUser3()` function turns off USER2 and calls `glowUser0()` only once with a `glowTime` delay. This completes the loop. The `glowUser0()` function will turn off the lit USER3 LED and turn on the USER0 LED. Then, it calls the `glowsUser1()` function with a delay of 100 milliseconds. This way, the loop continues.

7. While this loop is going on, the `exitTimer` event is counting time in parallel. It will trigger after 30 seconds. The `exitProgram()` function will be called. It will turn off all the LEDs and clear `tempTimer`. As nothing is left for execution, the program will exit.

Dancing LEDs in both directions

Let's create another illusion program where the light will go from USER0 to USER3. Then, instead of starting again from USER0, it travels back in the opposite direction from USER3 to USER0. We will follow the turning on of the LED sequence: USER0 -> USER1 -> USER2 -> USER3 -> USER2 -> USER1 -> USER0, and so on. This will look like the LED is traveling till the edge and then bouncing back. Type the previous danceLEDs.js program as it is. Change the following line in the glowUser3() function:

```
tempTimer = setTimeout(glowUser0, glowTime);
```

Replace it with the following line:

```
tempTimer = setTimeout(glowReverseUser2, glowTime);
```

Then, insert the following code after the glowUser3() function ends and before the exitProgram() function starts. Save the modified code as danceLEDs2.js and run it. You should see the LED pattern moving from USER0 to USER3 and then back to USER0:

```
function glowReverseUser2()
{
  b.digitalWrite("USR3",b.LOW);
  b.digitalWrite("USR2", b.HIGH);
  tempTimer =setTimeout(glowReverseUser1,glowTime);
}

function glowReverseUser1()
{
  b.digitalWrite("USR2",b.LOW);
  b.digitalWrite("USR1", b.HIGH);
  tempTimer = setTimeout(glowUser0,glowTime);
}
```

Program explanation

Two new functions are added: glowReverseUser2() and glowReverseUser1(). When the regular glow sequence goes from USER0 to the USER3 LED, instead of calling glowUser0(), we call the glowReverseUser2() function. So, instead of starting from USER0 LED again, our program takes a reverse direction to glow the USER2 LED. The glowReverseUser2() function calls glowReverseUser1(), which glows the USER1 LED. When the reverse sequence hits the USER0 LED, it will follow the normal USER0 to USER3 sequence again.

This whole program has many small functions. It is necessary because `setTimeout()` needs a block of code kept in the function to continue after timeout. One could argue that the same result can be achieved by combining similar functions in a single function with few arguments and a switch-case pattern inside. It will reduce the code length but that will hamper the simplicity of our program. We will do it in the next chapter while dancing external LEDs.

Summary

In this chapter, we wrote and tested a few BoneScript programs. We used Arduino-like functions to blink onboard LEDs. We learned how to exit the program automatically after some time and run your program without the Cloud9 IDE. Finally, we wrote a program to dance the LEDs in a single direction and in both directions. All these programs are done without attaching any external component to BeagleBone. In the next chapter, we will connect external LEDs to BeagleBone and write similar programs to blink/dance them.

3
Blinking External LEDs

In the previous chapter we programmed onboard LEDs on BeagleBone using BoneScript APIs. As BeagleBone is an embedded device, it can be used in an environment where a keyboard, mouse and monitor might not be available. Rather, most of the times embedded boards do not have these devices. Typical input and output components of embedded boards are LEDs and push-buttons. LEDs can be used as the output device to represent information, for example the board may turn an LED on when there is high system load and turn it off when the system load is low. So, by looking at LEDs we get information about if the system is under high load or not. That is why it is important to program LEDs on BeagleBone so that we can send information as output via LEDs where the monitor is absent. In this chapter, we will continue to program LEDs. We will connect external LEDs and blink them using our BoneScript program. To achieve this, we need to learn about GPIO on BeagleBone.

Here are the topics that will be covered in this chapter:

- What is GPIO?
- BeagleBone GPIO map
- Blinking external LED circuit setup
- Program to blink external LED
- Dancing external LEDs circuit setup
- Program to dance external LEDs

What is GPIO?

The BeagleBone processor AM335X has several pins to communicate with outside chips and components. Some of these are dedicated pins to communicate with the DDR memory chip on BeagleBone. These pins are permanently connected to a memory chip. You cannot attach other components or chips to these pins. The same holds true for the processor's JTAG pins, USB pins, Power IC connection pins, etc. These pins have a fixed role of communicating with respective components/chips. These types of pins dedicated to communicate with single component/chip are specific purpose pins. Users do not have control over these pins individually. The processor with all its pins as specific purpose pins becomes rigid. It becomes less flexible to attach new components and program them.

To provide flexibility to adopt components outside the board, some of the digital pins on the processor are not given any specific role. Users are given the power to control each one of them via software. These pins with no specific role are called **GPIO (General Purpose Input Output)**. The following features define a digital pin as GPIO:

- The user can enable or disable it by program. This can be done at run time.

- The user can set the direction of a pin as input or output according to the type of attached component. Only one direction can be active at a time. Once selected, the pin will operate in that direction only. The user can change direction at run time. We have seen the function `PinMode()` in the previous chapter, which sets the direction.

- When the direction is set as output, the GPIO pin can be set as HIGH or LOW. Accordingly, the connected chip/component gets turned on or off. Changing the pin as HIGH and LOW in pattern can send digital data or control signals through the pin. We have seen the function `digitalWrite()` to write on an output pin in the previous chapter.

- When set as input, a GPIO pin reads digital signals coming from a connected component/chip. It can be HIGH or LOW. Digital data or control signals can be interpreted based on HIGH and LOW patterns collected over time. Often processor interrupt (irq) is configurable when GPIO work as input. We will learn about GPIO input in the next chapter.

The user can attach various digital components to a GPIO pin like external LEDs, buttons, buzzers, relays, and so on. They allow the connection of components that are not a default part of the board, for example BeagleBone does not come with an infrared sensor. But you can attach an infrared sensor to a GPIO pin and capture infrared signals.

GPIO is a feature provided by a processor. Embedded board manufacturers might use some of the available GPIO pins for specific purposes like showing status via LEDs, monitoring SD card insertion/removal, resetting an external chip, for example the onboard USER3 LED on BeagleBone is actually connected to processor pin GPIO1_24. Drivers to handle GPIO pins are written generically. At the time of booting, the BeagleBone hardware description device tree file informs the kernel that GPIO1_24 is actually an LED. We will learn about the device tree in detail in the *Appendix C, Pinmux and the Device Tree*. Even after using some GPIO pins for a specific purpose, BeagleBone has plenty of GPIO pins left to be controlled by the user. Let's see how BeagleBone gives us access to GPIO pins and how to program them.

BeagleBone GPIO map

BeagleBone has two expansion headers at both edges with 46 pins each. If you look carefully, you can see that headers are marked as P8, P9 and pins 1, 2, 45, and 46 are marked on the board. Not all extension pins are GPIOs. Some pins are reserved to deal with analog components. Some pins are power and ground pins. BeagleBone SRM and Schematic diagram give details of which extension pin is connected to which of the processor pin. Many sensors/components require an external power supply to operate. Power supply can be given to these sensors via power and ground pins. BeagleBone provides both 3.3 volts and 5 volts pins to power up sensors with that voltage level.

The AM335X processor has four banks of 32 GPIO pins each. Not all 128 pins are accessible. Some are used for a specific purpose like USER LEDs. Please refer to the image below to see the list of GPIOs available on extension headers of BeagleBone Black. A total of 32 GPIO pins are available to users on BeagleBone Black. BeagleBone White and BeagleBone Green have the same pins with some extra pins available for GPIO. The bone101 webpage seen in the *Chapter 1, Cloud9 IDE* gives a correct listing of GPIO pins for respective BeagleBone versions:

Note that extension port numbers and numbers in GPIO names are different. We will be using extension numbers in our programs. So there is no need to learn mapping with GPIO names. You can get GPIO name mapping in BeagleBone SRM.

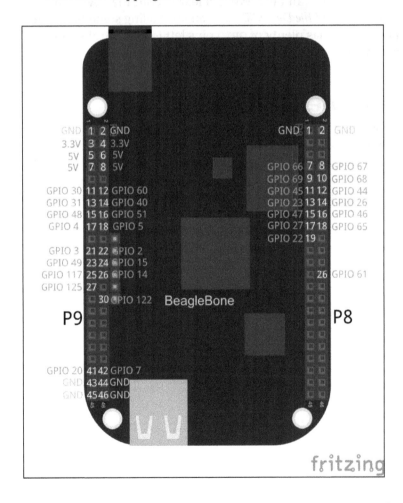

BeagleBone Black came with additional features of HDMI and emmc storage compared with old BeagleBone White. They needed some pins to communicate with the BeagleBone processor. Pins 3–6 and 20–25 and pins 27–46 on P8 headers were given to HDMI and emmc to communicate with the processor. Though it is not visible outside, these pins on P8 headers are shared with HDMI/emmc internally. That is why BeagleBone Black has a smaller number of GPIOs available than BeagleBone White and BeagleBone Green. Using pins that are internally connected to HDMI will cause the HDMI output to be disrupted. If you need to use more than 32 GPIOs, you can disable HDMI/emmc using a device tree and use freed pins. This is covered in the *Appendix C, Pinmux and the Device Tree*.

GPIO pins are an interface between the BeagleBone processor and the external world. Consider a USB-based fan attached to a desktop computer. In that case, communication is done from the processor to the USB controller and from the USB controller to the USB fan. Over-voltage and over-current damages the USB controller only. But when an LED is connected to a BeagleBone GPIO pin, communication happens directly in between the BeagleBone processor and LED. Over-voltage and over-current to these pins can damage the processor directly. Let's put the warning again.

BeagleBone works on 3.3 volts logic level. Do not connect a component that works with logic level (e.g. 5V) to these pins. It can damage the circuit or the board itself. If a component is using another logic level like 5V, you need to use a level shifter in between.

Blinking external LED circuit setup

Until now, we have dealt with onboard LEDs only, which require no extra component connected. In our next exercise, we are going to connect an external LED to BeagleBone. This requires a few components. You can get these easily in a local electronics shop or online websites like sparkfun or mouser:

- **LED** – We need a single LED for this exercise. An LED is actually a **Light Emitting Diode**. They allow flowing current in one direction only. When current passes through them, they glow. When connected in the opposite direction, no current is passed through.

- **Male-to-male jumper wires** – We need jumper wires to connect BeagleBone and components through a breadboard.

- **400Ω–1kΩ resistor** – Passing too much current through an LED can damage it. So, there is a need to put a resistor to reduce the current. In our case, we need any resistor inside the range 400Ω-1kΩ.

- **Half-size breadboard** – Creating a circuit of components requires soldering work. For circuit modification and reusing components, you need to do de-soldering as well. Someone with no soldering experience can find this tedious. A breadboard provides a hassle-free way to create solderless circuit for quick testing. A breadboard has many interconnected pin holes. You can plug components into a breadboard and create a temporary circuit. A circuit created using a breadboard is easily modifiable. Here is a diagram to show interconnection inside a breadboard. Pins at the edges are column-connected. Pins in the middle are row-connected. You have to keep interconnection in mind before creating a circuit:

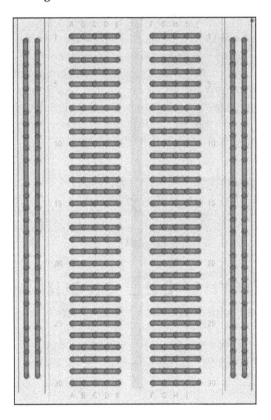

Now, power off the board and disconnect the power and USB cable. Then attach components to BeagleBone as shown in the next diagram:

1. Locate the 10 number pin on the P8 expansion header on BeagleBone. Let's call it P8_10 pin. Plug one end of the male to male jumper cable (yellow color) here. Put another end to any free row-connected hole in the breadboard.

2. Plug one end of the resistor in the breadboard hole inside the same row that we plugged the yellow cable. Now, the P8_10 and resistor are connected. Put another end of the resistor so that you jump across another row that is not connected. Please refer to the diagram below for this. There is no positive or negative end for the resistor. You can connect any end to positive, and any end to negative.

3. An LED has positive and negative ends. You need to connect the positive end to the positive side and the negative end to the negative side of the circuit. An LED's positive pin leg is always longer than the negative pin leg. Attach the positive end of the LED in the hole from the row we connected to the other side of the resistor in the last step. Now, P8_10 is connected to the positive side of the LED through the resistor. Connect the negative end of the LED to any other free row-connected hole on breadboard.

4. Plug one end of the black jumper cable in the same row that we plugged the negative end of the LED. Plug another end to pin number 2 on the P8 header. Let's call it P8_2 pin. Now, P8_2 pin is connected to the negative end of the LED.

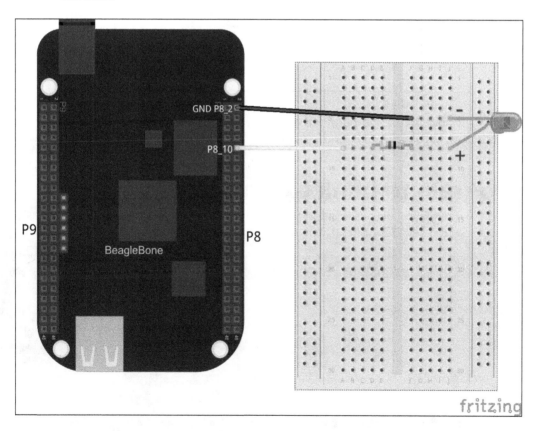

Circuit analysis

GPIO pin P8_10 is connected to the positive end of the LED through the resistor. The resistor is reducing current to protect the LED. The negative end of the LED is connected to pin P8_2. Pin P8_2 is actually a ground/negative pin. When P8_10 is HIGH, the current will flow from positive P8_10 to ground P8_2. It will flow through the LED and it will glow. When P8_10 will be LOW, both P8_10 and P8_2 will have no voltage. So, there will be no current flow and the LED will be off.

What we did ultimately can fit into this circuit diagram:

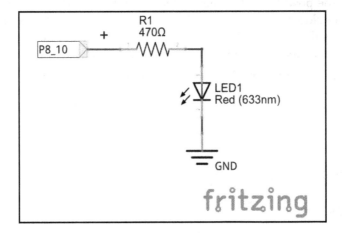

The LED in this circuit will blink if the voltage at P8_10 node is turned on and off periodically. Let's write a program to do so.

Program to blink external LED

Now that everything is connected, type the following program in Cloud9, save it as blinkExternalLED.js and run. You should be able to see the LED blinking each second:

```
var b = require('bonescript');
var led = "P8_10";
var state = b.HIGH;
var loopTime = 1000;
var exitTime = 30000;

b.pinMode(led, b.OUTPUT);
b.digitalWrite(led, state);

var loopTimer = setInterval(blink, loopTime);
```

```
var exitTimer = setTimeout(exitProgram,exitTime);

function blink()
{
    if(state == b.LOW) state = b.HIGH;
    else state = b.LOW;
    b.digitalWrite(led, state);
}

function exitProgram()
{
    b.digitalWrite(led,b.LOW);
    clearInterval(loopTimer);
}
```

Explanation

This is the exact same program that we did in the previous chapter except we put LED as string P8_10 here. We declared P8_10 pin direction as output using function pinMode(). When our program does digitalWrite() HIGH on P8_10 pin, the processor puts 3.3V on that pin. The current starts flowing from P8_10 to P8_2 and the LED glows. When the program writes LOW, the processor puts 0V on P8_10. As both ends have no voltage, the current flow stops and our LED goes off. When we do this in a repeating time interval, the external LED blinks. You can replace the LED in the above circuit with a buzzer to get sound notification. You can use a relay switch to ON/OFF AC devices in the home by connecting the relay to the GPIO pin.

Troubleshooting

1. Do not connect both ends of an LED or resistor on a breadboard such that they become electrically interconnected.

2. If the LED is not blinking, check if the resistor, LED and jumper pins are correctly fitting in breadboard pin holes. If needed, remove all jumper pins, LED and resistor. Connect everything again correctly. Please make sure that you are using the correct pins for connection – P8_2 and P8_10.

3. If you use different colors for jumper wires, it becomes easy to understand and debug. Black wire is used to connect with ground as convention. Red wire is used to connect a positive power source. We are using yellow/green wires for the GPIO.

4. Change the LED and check. Sometimes they blow out.

5. You can check the voltage across LED pins using a multimeter to find out if there is a broken circuit in between.

Dancing external LEDs circuit setup

Let's write a program to dance LEDs in both directions like we did in the previous chapter. For this exercise, you will need:

- **Seven LEDs**: We are using seven LEDs to create a dancing pattern
- **Male-to-male jumper wires**: We need jumper wires to connect BeagleBone and components through a breadboard
- **Seven resistor 400Ω–1kΩ**: A resistor is needed to limit current flowing through an LED to protect it.
- **Half size breadboard**: A breadboard is needed to create a solderless circuit.

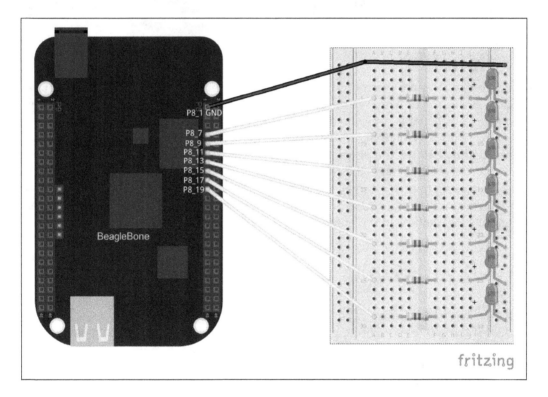

Power off the board and disconnect the power and USB cable. Then attach components to BeagleBone as shown in the previous diagram.

Circuit analysis

This circuit is the same as the last circuit repeated seven times. We used seven GPIO pins to connect seven LEDs through resistors. These pins are P8_7, P8_9, P8_11, P8_13, P8_15, P8_17 and P8_19. The negative end of all LEDs is connected to a single column. This column is connected to ground via P8_1 pin on BeagleBone. So, seven different positive ends are connected to common ground. When P8_7 pin is HIGH, the first LED will turn on. Then if P8_9 is turned HIGH and P8_7 LOW, it will look like the LED glow has shifted from the first LED to the second and so on.

Program to dance external LEDs in both directions

Write the following program in Cloud9 and save it as danceExternalLEDs.js. Run it and you should see dancing LEDs in both directions:

```
var b = require('bonescript');
var loopTime = 50;
var exitTime = 20000;
var reverse_direction;
var index;
var LEDs = ["P8_7","P8_9","P8_11","P8_13","P8_15","P8_17","P8_19"];

for(index in LEDs)
{
    b.pinMode(LEDs[index],b.OUTPUT);
}

index=0;
var loopTimer = setInterval(danceLEDs, loopTime);
var exitTimer = setTimeout(exitProgram,exitTime);

function danceLEDs()
{
    switch(index)
    {
        case 0:
            b.digitalWrite(LEDs[index+1],b.LOW);
            b.digitalWrite(LEDs[index++],b.HIGH);
            reverse_direction = false;
             break;
        case (LEDs.length-1):
            b.digitalWrite(LEDs[index-1],b.LOW);
```

```
                b.digitalWrite(LEDs[index--],b.HIGH);
                reverse_direction = true;
                break;
          default:
                if(reverse_direction == true)
                {
                    b.digitalWrite(LEDs[index+1],b.LOW);
                    b.digitalWrite(LEDs[index--],b.HIGH);
                }
                else
                {
                    b.digitalWrite(LEDs[index-1],b.LOW);
                    b.digitalWrite(LEDs[index++],b.HIGH);
                }
        }
    }
}

function stopTimer()
{
    for(index in LEDs)
    {
        b.digitalWrite(LEDs[index],b.LOW);
    }
    clearTimeout(tempTimer);
}
```

 It might take long time to get output of this program sometimes when BeagleBone does device tree adjustment internally. You can confirm that by checking /var/log/messages file on BeagleBone.

Explanation

First we declared an array of strings and named it LEDs. We initialized it with names of all attached GPIO pins sequentially. The for(index in LEDs) code iterates over all elements in array LEDs and sets the direction of each GPIO pin to output. We set the exitTime timer to call the exitProgram() function after 20 seconds. It will turn off an LED if any one is left turned on and exit the program. Then we set the loopTime timer to call the danceLEDs() function after each 50 milliseconds.

Inside the danceLEDs() function, we consider four different cases based on the value of the global variables index and reverse_direction:

1. If index = 0 then we turn the first GPIO pin(P8_7) to HIGH. This will glow the first LED. Then we increment the index and break the loop. After 50 milliseconds, danceLED() will be called again.

2. If 0 < index < 7 (length of array) and reverse_direction flag is not set, then turn the current array index GPIO to HIGH and turn the previous array index GPIO to LOW. Then we increment the index and break the loop. This will create a glowing LED illusion from the second LED until the last LED.

3. If index = 7, then turn the last GPIO pin (p8_19) to HIGH and the previous GPIO (P8_17) to LOW. This will create a glowing LED illusion from the second to last LED to the last LED. The variable index is decremented here and the flag reverse_direction is set.

4. If 0 < index < 7 and reverse_direction flag is set, then turn the current array index GPIO to HIGH and turn the next array index GPIO to LOW. Then we decrement the index and break the loop. This creates a glowing LED illusion in the reverse direction (from the last LED till 1st LED). When control reaches the first LED, the reverse_direction flag is cleared and we are into the index = 0 case again.

Function danceLEDs() works on members of LEDs array. We have not hard-coded values. If we add another GPIO pin as a new member in the LEDs array, the program will still consider newly added pins and iterate through all array members. That means we can extend this program to more LEDs. All you need to do is connect a new LED to free GPIO pins physically and add their names in LEDs array in the program. You can replace the LEDs' array initialization line with the following to get the same glowing pattern on USER LEDs:

```
var LEDs = ["USR0","USR1","USR2","USR3"];
```

Troubleshooting steps for this program are the same as for the previous program.

Summary

In this chapter we learned that GPIO pins are digital pins which provide control to the user to turn it on/off and set input/output direction via software. When the pin direction is set to output, one can make it HIGH/LOW and the component attached to that pin gets that HIGH/LOW signal. GPIO pins provide plug-in functionality to add external digital components to BeagleBone. We found that BeagleBone provides many GPIO pins via P8 and P9 headers to which we can connect digital components like LEDs, buzzers, relays, and so on. Then we wrote and tested BoneScript programs to blink and dance external LEDs. Now, we will move to interaction with another electronic component – the push button. In the next chapter, we will be taking input from the push button and respond.

4

Controlling LED Using
a Push Button

In the previous chapter, we wrote programs that were instructing LEDs to be on or off in pattern. LEDs are output devices. BeagleBone provides some information to us through LEDs, for example, by default the USER1 LED is turned on when the SD card is accessed. Sometimes, we want to give some information to BeagleBone, such as send an e-mail or send SMS. We need to use an input electronic component that will pass our information to BeagleBone. The most common input component used in the embedded world is the push button. BeagleBone has three small push buttons onboard. But they are already assigned to system critical work. So, we will use an external push button to convey our message to BeagleBone in this chapter.

Here are the topics that will be covered in this chapter:

- Reading from digital components
- Push button circuit setup
- Program to read from push button
- Reading via interrupts
- Push button LED circuit setup
- Program to control LED by push button

Reading from digital components

Push buttons are digital. They are either pressed or released. There are some touch buttons that work just like push buttons. They generate a HIGH signal when touched. There are some sensors that work as HIGH/LOW digital input devices. They just give information if the threshold value is reached or not. For example, some IR sensors come with a digital pin that gives only a HIGH/LOW value if it detects an obstacle in between a specific distance. Any electronic device capable of generating a HIGH/LOW signal can be treated as an input device. This signal is sensed at the connected BeagleBone pin and the input value is interpreted as HIGH/LOW. These are all digital input devices.

The BoneScript library provides the function digitalRead() to read from digital components. The function digitalRead() requires the pin to be initialized first using the function pinMode() similar to digitalWrite(). But it should be initialized for *input* unlike digitalWrite(). Here is the prototype of the digitalRead() function:

```
digitalRead( pin, callback)
```

The parameters are as follows:

- pin: The BeagleBone pin identifier string
- callback: Name of function which will be called automatically when digitalRead() finishes.

The function digitalRead() internally reads from the sysfs file that corresponds to the pin. This may take some time to return and the Node will be blocked until then. This is a blocking function and needs to be done in an asynchronous way. So, the second parameter is a callback function that will be called automatically when digitalRead() completes. This callback function gets called with a special object as parameter. This special object has the property value, which tells us if the pin is HIGH or LOW. This is much like a structure and its member if you are coming from a C background. You will get a clear idea once you go through the program. Before writing the program, we need to set up a circuit for the program.

Push button circuit setup

For this exercise, we will need:

- **4-pin push button**: A push button is an electronic component that is attached to two points in a circuit. It is also called a tact switch. When it is pressed, it joins these two points and the circuit is completed. The circuit is disconnected when the button is not pressed.

- **Male-to-male jumper wires**: We need jumper wires to connect BeagleBone and components through a breadboard.

- **Half-size breadboard**: A breadboard is needed to create a solderless circuit.

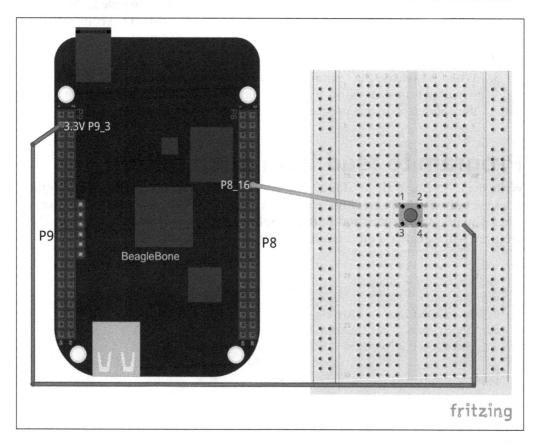

Power off the board and attach the components to BeagleBone as shown in the preceding diagram.

Circuit analysis

Let's see the analysis step by step:

1. The 4-pin push button is divided into two sides. Within the first side, pole 1 and pole 2 are already connected. Another side has pole 3 and pole 4 connected. But these both sides are not connected to each other. When the button is pressed, the pole 1 and pole 2 side gets connected to the pole 3 and pole 4 side.

2. Pin P9_3 and P9_4 are not regular GPIO pins but provide continuous 3.3 voltage. They are useful to provide voltage to electronics components. Here, we apply 3.3V to pole 4 and the current is stuck there until the button is pressed. Once the button is pressed, pole 4 is connected to pole 1. We have joined pole 1 to P8_16, which is in input mode. The circuit get completed and current starts flowing from P9_3 to P8_16. If we read pin P8_16 now, we will get the value HIGH.

3. When we release the button, pole 1 and pole 4 are disconnected and the circuit gets broken. Now, if we read pin P8_16 from our program, we will get the value LOW. In our program, we will print whatever value we find.

Program to read from push button

Write the following code in Cloud9 and save it as pushButton.js. Run the program, keep the button pressing and releasing. You should see **Button is pressed** printed when you press the button and **Button is released** when the button is released. The program will exit after a minute automatically.

```
var b = require('bonescript');var loopTime = 1000;
var exitTime = 60000;
var button = 'P8_16';
b.pinMode(button, b.INPUT);
var loopTimer = setInterval(check,loopTime);
var exitTimer = setTimeout(exitProgram,exitTime);

function check()
{
  b.digitalRead(button, checkButton);
}

function checkButton(pinObj)
{
  if(pinObj.value == b.HIGH)
  {
    console.log("Button is pressed");
  }
  else
  {
    console.log("Button is released");
  }
}

function exitProgram()
```

```
    {
        clearInterval(loopTimer);
        console.log("Program exiting");
    }
```

Explanation

We first declared that we are going to use the P8_16 pin as the input. That means we will only read from it and not write on it. We set the timer exitTimer to call the function exitProgram() after a minute. Then we set the timer to call the function check() after every second. Inside the function check(), we are calling digitalRead(). In the first parameter, we are specifying that reading is to be done on the 16th pin on the P8 extension header. In the second parameter, we are specifying to call function checkButton() when reading is done. When reading is done, checkButton() will be called with a parameter of type object. We named it pinObj. Inside the checkButton() function, we are checking if the property value of object pinObj is HIGH or not and print accordingly. If the button is pressed when this checking is going on, BeagleBone senses 3.3V at P8_16 and pinObj.value matches to HIGH and our program prints **Button is pressed**. If something goes bad, the pinObj.err property is set with error information. You can print it for debugging. If there is no error, it is set to undefined.

There is a need to add a pull-down resistor at **pole 1** for a reliable output. We are not including it to avoid complexity. Instead of printing, we can glow the LED like we did in previous chapter. In that case, the LED will glow when we press the button and will turn off when the button is released. We are going to write a program to achieve this soon.

Reading via interrupts

In our last program, we were checking if the button is pressed or not after each second. The button must remain pressed at the time of console printing to get it printed pressed. If you press the button quickly in between two printings, it will still print released. So in this situation, one button press event is lost. Consider another scenario. It is possible that nobody pressed the button for a long time. But still the program will wake up every 1 second and check for pin values. This is called **polling**. It wastes lots of CPU time and system resources on repetitive checking. This is not good programming practice. Polling prevents the CPU from going to sleep and saves power. This is not good for embedded systems where the battery power is crucial. Also, you cannot respond well to high frequency input signals using polling.

To solve this problem, some I/O devices/components are allowed to notify the CPU when a specific event occurs. These events are like a touch being sensed on a touchscreen or data copying being done or a device being attached to the USB port or the button is pressed. Some physical connection lines are reserved for this. I/O devices send notification signals on these lines to the CPU. This whole mechanism is called **interrupt**. With this mechanism in place, there is no need for the CPU to check the device for event information again and again. The CPU can do other work relying on the component/device and interrupt controller for notification of an event. The saved CPU time can be used to do better multitasking or going into sleep mode to save power. We often use interrupt a service without being aware of using it, for example, when the power button is pressed, an interrupt signal is sent to the processor, which gets handled by the OS to perform an orderly shutdown.

BeagleBone has a dedicated interrupt controller tightly coupled with the CPU, which handles interrupts. No event is lost because the interrupt controller makes sure every notification goes till CPU. When we want a button press event to be notified to the CPU via interrupt, there is a need to interrupt support on the GPIO pin to which the button is connected. When the direction is set to input, all GPIO pins on BeagleBone can generate interrupts. This is supported in the Linux kernel as well as at software level. BeagleBone supports interrupt generation when the input signal changes from LOW to HIGH (RISING) or from HIGH to LOW (FALLING) or in both cases (CHANGE). The input signal is RISING at the time of pushing button and FALLING at the time of the pressed button getting released. We can register our interrupt handler function for any of these events RISING / FAILING / CHANGE. Later when events occur, OS will be notified and our interrupt handler function will be called. This way, we will never miss any quick button presses and unnecessary wake ups & checks will be avoided.

BoneScript provides the function attachInterrupt() and detachInterrupt() which make use of the GPIO interrupt mechanism internally. The function attachInterrupt() maps specified events/modes on the specified pin to interrupt handler function. The handler function gets called when that event occurs on that pin. The function detachInterrupt() unmaps this binding. Here are prototypes of these functions:

- attachInterrupt(pin, handler, mode, callback)

The parameters are as follows:

- ○ `pin`: The BeagleBone pin identifier string.

- ○ `handler`: Expression evaluating to `true` or `false`. Based on evaluation result, interrupt is handled or ignored. We will write `true` at this place in our program so that every interrupt generated associated with attached interrupt is handled with our handler.

- ○ `mode`: Event to consider when generating interrupt. Mode may be `RISING` or `FALLING` or `CHANGE`. You need to specify `RISING` if you want to be notified when button is pressed and specify `FALLING` if you want button-release notification. Specify mode as `CHANGE` if you want to consider both button pressed and released to be considered.

- ○ `callback`: This is the name of the interrupt handler function. This function will be called automatically when interrupt is generated for specified mode.

- detachInterrupt(pin, callback)

  The parameters are as follows:

  - ○ `pin` - BeagleBone pin identifier string.

  - ○ `callback` – Name of the function to be called upon completion of this function. Please note that this is an optional parameter. We are going to use `detachInterrupt()` without this parameter.

Before writing the program, we need to set up the circuit for the program.

Push button LED circuit setup

For this exercise, we will need:

- 4-pin push button
- Male-to-male jumper wires
- Half-size breadboard
- LED
- 470Ω resistor

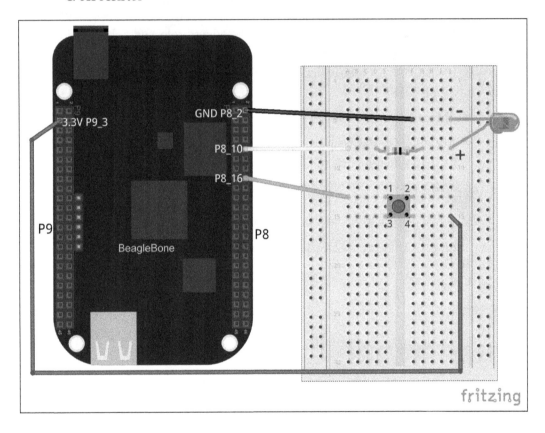

Power off the board and attach components to BeagleBone as shown in the preceding diagram.

Circuit analysis

This circuit is a combination of a push button circuit and the blinking LED circuit we studied earlier. P9_3, push-button and P8_16 create a push button input circuit. P8_10, LED and P8_1 create LED output circuit. Both circuits are independent. Our program listens to input circuit and responds on the output circuit.

Program to control LED by push button

Write the following code in it and save it as pushButton2.js. Run the program, keep button pressing and releasing. You should see the LED glowing when the button is pressed. When the button is released, the LED should be turned off.

```
var b = require('bonescript');
var inputPin = 'P8_16';
var outputPin = 'P8_10';

b.pinMode(inputPin, b.INPUT);
b.pinMode(outputPin, b.OUTPUT);
b.attachInterrupt(inputPin, true, b.CHANGE, interruptCallback);
var exitTimer = setTimeout(exitProgram, 60000);

function interruptCallback(pinObj)
{
  if(pinObj.value==b.HIGH)
  {
    b.digitalWrite(outputPin, b.HIGH);
  }
  else
  {
    b.digitalWrite(outputPin, b.LOW);
  }
}

function exitProgram()
{
  b.digitalWrite(outputPin, b.LOW);
  b.detachInterrupt(inputPin);
  console.log('Interrupt detached');
}
```

Explanation

We are using GPIO pin P8_16 as input from the push button and P8_10 as output to the LED. Then we attached interrupt on GPIO input pin P8_16 for the event CHANGE in current. The CHANGE mode means we will be called upon RISE or FALL in current. That means the interrupt will be generated when the button is pressed as well as when the button is released. We specified that the name of interrupt handler function is interruptCallback(). This callback function will be called automatically when the interrupt is generated related to pin P8_16. Then we made sure that the program ends after a minute with the exitProgram() function.

InterruptCallback() is called with a special object as parameter we named pinObj here. Object pinObj has a property value which is HIGH when the button is pressed. It becomes LOW when the button is released. If it is HIGH, we turn on the LED. If it is LOW, we turn off the LED. After a minute, exitTimer gets triggered and the function exitProgram() gets called. Inside it, we turn off the LED and detach the interrupt on input pin P8_16. Now, we are no longer notified if the button is pressed or released.

If you are not getting the desired output, you can insert console.log() before turning the LED on and off. You can also check if the number of interrupts count for gpiolib in /proc/interrupts file is increasing per button press. You can replace the LED ON/OFF code with buzzer speaker beeps or trigger/kill some processes for a more realistic scenario.

Summary

In this chapter, we programmed the most common digital input component—a push button. At first, we wrote a program to check whether the push button is pressed or not. We found that it is not efficient programming practice. So, we wrote a program that uses an interrupt mechanism. In that program, we read from the input push button and based on the input value we responded to the output LED. That was a minimal example of an interactive embedded system. A similar setup can be done with any digital input source such as a keypad, slide button, or touch button. A digital input source can also be a sensor/chip that sends ON/OFF data. In the next chapter, we will use BeagleBone's special capability to deal with analog components. This will open the gate to collect information from sensors.

5
Reading from Analog Sensors

We have dealt with digital components up to now. They have only two possible states: **ON** or **OFF**. Not all electronics components are digital. Many electronic components are analog. These types of components can have any value among the possible infinite values. Dealing with analog components is different to dealing with digital components. Most of the electronic sensors available are analog. In this chapter, we will write programs to deal with analog components: temperature sensor and light sensor.

In this chapter, we are going to cover these topics:

- Analog I/O
- Reading from analog components
- TMP36 temperature sensor circuit setup
- Program to print temperature
- LDR circuit setup
- Program to check light intensity

Analog I/O

In digital electronics, there are only two possible values—ON or OFF. In real life, we can not describe everything as ON or OFF. Many entities can have a wide range of values. For example, weight cannot be described as ON or OFF. You need to specify a number to describe magnitude of weight. Weight can be 66 kg. It can be 65.9 kg. It can be 65.93472641 kg. All these are valid numbers to describe weight. The possible values for analog entities are infinite, unlike with digital systems. The same holds true for analog entities like length, temperature, air pressure, and so on. If we plot a graph of values over time, we get an analog signal wave. The disadvantage of analog information is it's susceptible to noise and information is lost during transmission due to distortion, non-linearities, and so on.

Most of the sensors are of analog type. They get information from the environment. Often the information is a unit or a scalar value of the environmental entity. Then they convert that value into corresponding voltage and generate that voltage on its data output pin. For example, the weight sensor gets information about weight in kilograms. The more weight it detects, the more voltage is generated on the sensor's output pin. A typical analog sensor sends a continuous raw analog signal on an output pin. BeagleBone has dedicated pins to take analog input. BeagleBone can read sensor output voltage through analog input pins and we can convert it back to the original unit in our program. The datasheet of that sensor needs to be referred in order to find out it's voltage range and how to convert the measured voltage to the original unit. Based on the calculated unit value, BeagleBone can respond using output devices, such as a glowing red LED when a higher than expected temperature is measured or playing the next video when corresponding values are captured at the infrared sensor (which is sent by IR remote control).

Like all computer systems, BeagleBone is a digital system. It cannot work on analog information directly. The voltage generated at an analog input pin has to be converted to digital for the BeagleBone to understand it. BeagleBone has a built-in **Analog to Digital Converter (ADC)** that converts captured variable voltage to scaled digital values. So, we get more of a range of values than just HIGH or LOW.

Regular **General-Purpose Input/Output (GPIO)** pins are not capable of reading analog information and converting to digital. BeagleBone has dedicated seven pins that can read from analog devices. These pins are capable of taking input only. They cannot be used for output purposes. BeagleBone SRM mentions them as **AIN0-AIN6**. Please check the following diagram for more details. The P9 header has seven analog input pins. It also has VDD_ADC and GND_ADC pins. These are VDD (voltage source) and GND is used to create analog circuits. This VDD pin is different from P9_3/P9_4 VDD pins because it provides 1.8V only. This is because BeagleBone ADC works at 1.8V logic level:

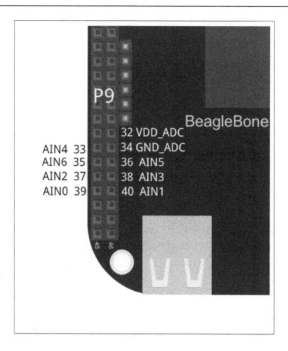

Warning

The BeagleBone ADC is capable of handling a maximum of 1.8V. It can get damaged if more voltage is given to analog input pins. Please read the sensor datasheet before you attach it to BeagleBone.

Reading from analog components

Digital components can fit in Boolean data type. Floating point data type is correct to describe analog values. BoneScript provides the function `analogRead()` to read the voltage at the analog pin. These pins are input-only. So, there is no need to initialize them using `pinMode()`. Here is the prototype of the `analogRead()` function:

```
analogRead(pin, callback)
```

The parameters of this function are described as follows:

- `pin`: BeagleBone pin identifier string
- `callback`: Name of function that will be called automatically when `analogRead()` finishes.

The first parameter `pin` is used to find the corresponding sysfs file to read data from. Similar to the `digitalRead()` function, the `analogRead()` function is *blocking*. It waits till analog voltage is read and the ADC conversion is done. The Node execution engine freezes till this happens. So, there is need for an asynchronous callback function. The second parameter is the callback function, which will be called automatically when `analogRead()` completes. Similar to `digitalRead()`, this callback function gets called with a special object as parameter. This special object has property *value*, which is the read value on the ADC. It is a floating point number between 0 and 1 where 0 is mapped to 0V and 1 is mapped to 1.8V. The mathematical function of this mapping is *f(x)=1.8x*. So, if you get the value 0.5, then voltage at the input pin is 0.9V. This conversion needs to be done for all read values. Getting the voltage value is not sufficient. You need to convert that to the corresponding sensor value. The sensor datasheet needs to be referred to in order do this conversion. Based on this information we will write program to print the temperature using the TMP36 temperature sensor. Let's make our BeagleBone aware of the outside temperature.

TMP36 temperature sensor circuit setup

For this exercise we need:

- **TMP36 sensor**

  The **TMP36** is temperature sensor created by a company named **Analog Devices**. It is easy to use and widely available. We get all the technical information about the TMP36 sensor in its datasheet. It is available at: `http://www.analog.com/en/mems-sensors/digital-temperature-sensors/tmp36/products/product.html`.

  TMP36 can measure temperature from -40°C to 125°C with a maximum ±2°C error. It is not good for checking human body temperature because the relative error is large enough to show bad health as good. But it is good in fire alarms, environment control systems, industrial process control systems, and so on. It needs 2.7V to 5.5V as input voltage to function. It gives output voltage 750mV at 25°C temperature. It has an output scale factor of 10mV/°C. So, it gives 0V at -50°C and increases with 10mV/°C. The voltage to Celsius temperature conversion equation for TMP36 is:

  *Temperature = 100 * Voltage(measured) - 50*

- **Male-to-male jumper wires**

  We need jumper wires to connect BeagleBone and components through a breadboard

- **Half-size breadboard**

  A breadboard is needed to create a solderless circuit

  Power off the board and attach components to BeagleBone as shown in the following diagram:

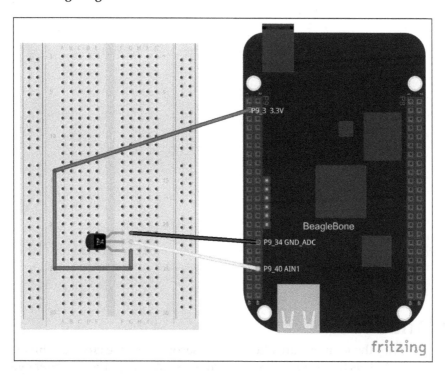

Circuit analysis

This circuit is a typical analog reading example. TMP36 has three leads. If you face the printed flat surface of the sensor, the left lead takes input voltage. We are providing 3.3V as input voltage to the left lead from **P9_3** pin. The right lead is the ground pin. We connect it to **P9_34**, which is the analog ground pin. The middle lead is giving the analog output voltage. We connect it to the analog input pin **P9_40**. If you connect TMP36 incorrectly and power on BeagleBone, it becomes hot. Please make sure it is connected correctly.

TMP36 is an analog sensor that generates analog voltage directly proportional to the temperature it detects. BeagleBone reads that voltage on the P9_40 analog input pin. BeagleBone ADC converts that analog value to the nearest digital value. We can read this value in our program using the `analogRead()` function. Then we can put that value in the equation to get the temperature. Let's write a program to do so.

Program to print temperature

Write the following code in Cloud9 and save it as `tmp36.js`. Run the program and check the printed temperature. Then touch the plastic body of the sensor for a few seconds (avoid touching metal pins). You should see an increase in temperature. The code for `tmp36.js` is as follows:

```
var b = require('bonescript');
var loopTimer = setInterval(readVoltageLoop, loopTime);
var loopTime = 2000;
var TMP36 = 'P9_40';

function readVoltageLoop()
{
   b.analogRead(TMP36, printTemperature);
}

function printTemperature(pinObj)
{
   var volt = pinObj.value * 1.8;
   var temperature = (100 * volt) - 50;
   console.log("Voltage at input pin = " + volt.toPrecision(3) + "
      Temperature in Celsius =" + temperature.toPrecision(3) );
}
```

Explanation

We want to print the temperature after every 2 seconds. So, we created a timer using `setInterval()`. This timer will call the function `readVoltageLoop()` after every 2 seconds. The function `readVoltageLoop()` calls `analogRead()` on pin `P9_40`. The first parameter specifies that reading is to be done on the 40th pin on the P9 extension header. This pin is connected to output pin of TMP36 which is sensing temperature from physical world. The second parameter specifies the callback function `printTemperature()` to be called when the analog reading is done. When reading is done, `printTemperature()` will be called with the parameter of type *object*. We named it `pinObj`. Inside the `printTemperature()` function, the property `value` of `pinObj` is the value read from ADC. This `value` is of float type inside 0 to 1 range. It needs to be converted to voltage. We use the mathematical mapping function seen earlier. We multiply the property `value` of `pinObj` by `1.8` and we get voltage sensed at pin `P9_40`. Then we follow the equation we got from the TMP36 datasheet to convert voltage to degrees Celsius temperature. We have seen that equation in the *TMP36 temperature sensor circuit setup* section previously. We get voltage and temperature in float data type with a long trail. We formatted it to a human readable format using the JavaScript method `toPrecision()`.

Here, it rounds off numbers and fits it in three-digit length. The + sign inside `console.log()` does string concatenation. After 2 seconds, the function `readVoltageLoop()` gets called again. It calls `printTemperature()` again. The function `printTemperature()` prints the sensed voltage and temperature. The program will run forever until exited manually. You can also use another popular temperature sensor **LM35** from **Texas Instruments**. The only change in the equation is: *Temperature = 100 * Voltage(measured)*. Now that we made our BeagleBone aware of the outside temperature, let's make it aware of the light intensity outside.

LDR circuit setup

To set up a **light dependent resistor (LDR)** circuit, we'll need:

- **LDR**

  An LDR is also called a **photocell** or **photoresistor**. It is special type of resistor. Its resistance decreases as it is exposed to light. The higher the light exposure, the lower the resistance. In a dark room, it has highest resistance. This property comes from physical characteristics of semiconductors used inside. LDR does not belong to a specific company. There is no official datasheet either. You can refer to this webpage for more information about LDR: `https://learn.adafruit.com/photocells`

- **Male-to-male jumper wires**

  We need jumper wires to connect BeagleBone and components through a breadboard

- **Half-size breadboard**

  A breadboard is needed to create solderless circuit

- **10KΩ resistor**

  A resistor is needed to create a voltage divider circuit

Power off the board and attach components to BeagleBone as shown in the following diagram:

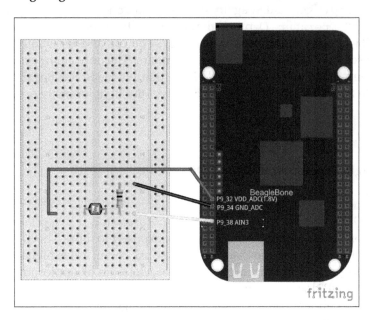

Circuit analysis

The resultant circuit schematic looks like this:

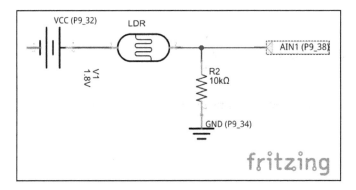

This circuit is a typical example of a *voltage divider* circuit. The input voltage is getting distributed among two routes reaching to ground/drain. Measuring light intensity through the LDR is easy. If the input voltage is applied on one end of the LDR, the other end will have measurable output voltage directly proportional to light intensity. When a 1.8V input is applied, the LDR scales the output voltage to the nearby input voltage value (close to 1.8V). There is a very small difference in output voltage generated by strong light and output voltage generated by low light. So, it becomes difficult to differentiate between high and low light intensity. Consider the preceding circuit without a **R2** resistor and no **GND** pin **P9_34**. Then the voltage at **P9_38** will be close to 1.8V even at low light and it will be difficult to detect a low light condition. This excessive output voltage has to be scaled down to be able to differentiate between light intensities. To reduce the magnitude of the output voltage, we added a **R2** resistor connected to ground. This is called voltage dividing. Now, the circuit starts at one end but finishes at two different ends. The LDR output voltage is divided among two routes. Excess voltage passes through the **R2** resistor. This reduced the voltage scales long range to distinguish low light and strong light situations. In our circuit, we have connected a 1.8V input voltage source at one end of the LDR. When the LDR is put in the dark, its resistance will increase and the output voltage at the other end will decrease. When the LDR is put near a bright light source, the resultant voltage at the other end will increase. BeagleBone reads that voltage on the **P9_38** analog input pin. BeagleBone ADC converts that analog value to the nearest digital value. We will read this in our program using the analogRead() function. Let's write a program to do so.

Program to check light intensity

Write the following code in Cloud9 and save it as ldr.js. Run the program and check the output voltage. If the LDR is exposed to bright sunlight, you may get the output message— **Looks like a bright sunny day**. If this is not possible, point a torch on the LDR surface. You should see the voltage has increased. Based on voltage value, you can guess the light brightness and respond by sending an SMS/e-mail or turn on a smart bulb in case of low light condition. You can also change the intensity of bulb according to the light intensity detected. The code for ldr.js is as follows:

```
var b = require('bonescript');
var loopTime = 2000;
var LDR = 'P9_38';
var loopTimer = setInterval(readVoltageLoop, loopTime);

function readVoltageLoop()
{
```

```
    b.analogRead(LDR, printVoltage);
}

function printVoltage(pinObj)
{
  var volt = pinObj.value * 1.8;
  console.log("Voltage at input pin = " + volt.toPrecision(3));
  if( volt > 1.6 )
  {
    console.log("Looks like bright sunny day");
  }
}
```

Explanation

We set the timer to call the function `readVoltageLoop()` on pin `P9_38` after every 2 seconds. Inside the `readVoltageLoop()` function, we called `analogRead()`. We specified the callback function `printVoltage()` to be called when the analog reading is done. So, when `analogRead()` finishes, `printVoltage()` is called with the parameter `pinObj`. The object `pinObj` has the property `value` that tells us the value read from the ADC. This value is float type inside the 0–1 range. We multiplied it by `1.8` to get the voltage sensed at pin P9_38. Then we used the JavaScript method `toPrecision()` to format the float value to a three-digit value and printed it. When this value is high, the LDR is facing bright light. When the value is low, the LDR is in a dark area.

Summary

In this chapter, we learned a little theory about the analog world. We saw analog pins available on BeagleBone. Then we wrote programs to measure temperature using temperature sensor TMP36. We also learned about LDR connections and wrote a program to measure light intensity. There is a big list of available analog sensors like accelerometers, sound sensors, gas detectors, piezoelectric pressure sensors, and so on. They can be interfaced with BeagleBone using circuits and programs we learned in this chapter. All you need to do is change the circuit/program according to the datasheet of that sensor. Now we know how to read from analog input devices. But we do not know how to write values on analog output devices. In the next chapter, we will learn a new concept called **Pulse Width Modulation (PWM)** and how it can be used to write on analog components/devices.

6
PWM – Writing Analog Information

In the previous chapter, we read information from analog sensors. It is time to write information on analog devices like motors. Writing analog information is not that straightforward. The BeagleBone processor has a **Pulse Width Modulation (PWM)** subsystem that can write analog information on some specific GPIO pins. In this chapter, we will learn how PWM works and how it can be used to interface analog output devices. Then we will write a program to fade an LED and drive a servo motor using PWM. In this chapter, will cover the following topics:

- What is PWM?
- BeagleBone's PWM
- Writing on analog components
- Fading LED circuit setup
- Program to fade in and fade out an LED
- Micro servo motor circuit setup
- Program to control micro servo motor

What is PWM?

Typically variable voltage is generated by analog circuits. Digital circuits generate only HIGH (3.3V) or LOW (0V) voltage. Digital microprocessors/microcontrollers cannot produce analog voltages themselves. They need a **Digital to Analog Convertor (DAC)**. We have seen in the previous chapter that BeagleBone has a built-in ADC that converts captured analog voltage to a value. This raises our hope that BeagleBone might have a DAC to generate analog output voltage. But this is not true. Instead of providing a DAC, it uses a mechanism called PWM, which achieves similar results. Some of the GPIO digital pins are driven by BeagleBone's PWM subsystem. It can generate any voltage inside the 0V to 3.3V range on these pins.

Suppose that we have connected an analog output device DC motor to one of the GPIO pins on BeagleBone (with capacitor filter). The speed of a DC motor changes proportionally to the voltage applied. The more voltage applied, the higher the motor speed. The connected GPIO digital pin can produce only 0V or 3.3V. Now, if we turn that GPIO pin ON and OFF very fast for an equal amount of time, the analog device will output as if it received half of the regular GPIO pin voltage, for example, if we turn the GPIO pin ON (3.3V) for 5 millisecond and OFF (0V) for the next 5 milliseconds and keep this pattern ongoing, the connected motor will rotate at a speed equivalent to the speed it rotates at 1.65V (half of 3.3V). At the same time, if you check the voltage between the pin and ground, you will see 1.65 reading on the multimeter. That means we got an average 1.65V output even if the GPIO pin is capable of producing only 0V and 3.3V.

If we plot a graph of **Time** versus **Volt** in the previous example, it looks like the following diagram. In this diagram, there are multiple square wave cycles generated periodically. One total wave cycle time is called a **Period**. Here, the period is 10 milliseconds. In one second, there will be 100 such periods or wave cycles. So, the frequency is 100Hz here. The time for which the GPIO pin was kept ON is 5 milliseconds. This is half of the total wave cycle time or period. The percentage ratio of the time pin was kept ON to a period is called the **Duty Cycle**. In this case, the duty cycle is 50%. It can be calculated by the following equation:

*Duty Cycle Percentage = (Time pin is ON / Period) * 100*

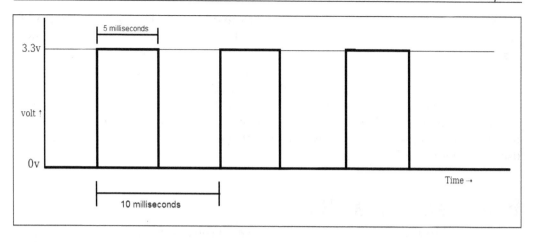

If we keep the period the same as 10 milliseconds and increase the time duration the pin was ON, then the duty cycle percentage will increase. The motor will have a 3.3 voltage supply for longer time than before. So, the average voltage will increase as well. The attached motor will spin faster than it was spinning before. Suppose we have increased the duty cycle up to 75%. The period is still 10 milliseconds. The frequency is still 100Hz. The time pin remaining ON is 7.5 milliseconds. In that case, we will get an output equivalent to 2.475V output on the analog circuit. If we increase the duty cycle further, we will get a more average voltage. But it will definitely be less than 3.3V. When the duty cycle is 100%, there will be no OFF time at all. We will get 3.3V voltage at the pin. This situation is the same as making that pin HIGH via digitalWrite(). If we decrease the duty cycle to less than 50% keeping the period fixed, we will get an average voltage between 0V and 1.65V. The 0% duty cycle will be the same as making that pin LOW via digitalWrite(). The average voltage can be calculated by the following equation:

Vavg = Vcc * Duty cycle

where *Vcc* = GPIO voltage level.

Thus by changing the duty cycle and keeping the period fix, we can simulate the output voltage inside the range 0V to 3.3V. This method of generating analog values on digital pins is called **Pulse Width Modulation (PWM)**. The name fits because these waves look like pulses and we are changing/modulating width. We also conclude that the average voltage is directly proportional to the duty cycle. Most of the time, we specify the duty cycle rather than the average output voltage.

PWM is more efficient than DAC. No digital to analog conversion is done in a PWM generation circuit. So, it reduces the need for extra analog components. Digital pins are reused here. There is no need for extra pins for analog output. PWM uses less power and generates less heat than DAC. This eliminates the need for heat sink. Also, PWM implementation is cheaper than DAC. PWM can be used to control DC motors, position servo motors, and control the luminance of LEDs. It is used in remote control devices. PWM is used in telecommunications to encode-decode data. It can be used almost all the time when an analog output is needed. It can even be used to generate audio signals.

BeagleBone's PWM

PWM can be implemented via program. One can write a program with `digitalWrite()` and `setInterval()` to create the desired frequency and desired duty cycle. But context switching and interrupts will make it inaccurate. Also, it will keep the CPU busy. The correct solution is to support this functionality at hardware level inside the CPU. The BeagleBone CPU has a **Pulse Width Modulation Subsystem (PWMSS)**, which allows the accurate creation of a PWM pattern without keeping the CPU busy. The CPU will be free to do other work while the PWM subsystem takes care of the PWM wave generation. This subsystem has control over only a few GPIO pins. It can switch output very fast on these pins and can control on/off timing. So, not all GPIO pins are capable of generating PWM.

PWMSS has a set of **Time Base Counter (TBCNT)** register and **Output Compare Register (OCR)** to generate the desired PWM pattern. OCRs are used to set the duty cycle. You can get detailed information about PWMSS in BeagleBone inside AM335X **Technical Reference Manual (TRM)**. BeagleBone has a total of eight PWM channels. These channels are driven by two types of PWM:

- **Enhanced High Resolution PWM (eHRPWM)**: There are three modules with two channels each. It has three PWM timer registers controlling six PWM channels. Two channels share the same timer. So, the duty cycle can be different but they both should be at the same frequency. It has a dedicated 16-bit time-base counter with period/frequency controls.

- **Enhanced Capture (eCAP)**—Though it is designed to capture modules, it can give auxiliary PWM output. It has a 32 bit timer base counter. This PWM type has two modules with one channel each.

Here is a diagram that shows the available PWM pins on BeagleBone Black.

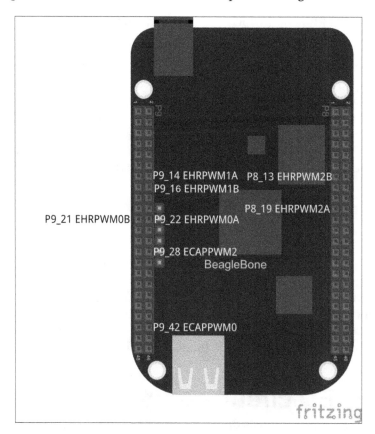

Writing on analog components

BoneScript provides the function `analogWrite()` to generate a PWM wave on any GPIO pin from the previous diagram. After a call to `analogWrite()`, the pin will generate PWM waves of a specified duty cycle. Here is the prototype of the `analogWrite()` function.

The code is as follows:

```
analogWrite(pin, value, [freq],[callback])
```

Where

`pin` – BeagleBone pin identifier string

`value` – duty cycle ratio of the PWM as value between `0` and `1`

`freq` – frequency of PWM in Hz

`callback` – name of function which will be called automatically when `analogWrite()` finishes.

Here, `freq` and `callback` parameters are optional. If `freq` is not specified, the default value 2 kHz is used. The duty cycle ratio value is not taken as a percentage but as a ratio between 0 to 1. It is a ratio of time it was ON to period. We can get that by dividing the percentage value by 100. So, a 50% duty cycle will be 0.5 value. Sometimes, you need to read the datasheet of the analog output device to find out the correct PWM values that it supports. Based on this information we will write a program to fade LEDs and control a micro servo motor.

[Do not use `pinMode()` for a pin on which you are calling `analogWrite()`. It forces the pin to be GPIO mode only.]

The function name seems like DAC functionality, but it just controls the PWM output. Though we are generating analog values inside the range, the signal is still digital. It is still capable of generating HIGH and LOW signals only. We are not controlling the voltage level. We are controlling the time digital signal is HIGH so that we generate any value as average value over the time. These are square digital waves. If you apply a low pass filter to them, you will get an analog sine wave.

Fading LED circuit setup

Though we have studied LEDs as digital devices, they are not actually digital devices. They emit light as per voltage put across them. If the voltage is high, they emit more light. If we provide an LED with a digital value, it will be ON or OFF. It will either light up with full brightness or not at all. If we provide intermediate values, it will still glow. But not with its full intensity. As we can apply any voltage between 0V to 3.3V using PWM on an LED now, we can change the brightness of the LED from lowest to highest and from highest to lowest. This will look like the LED is fading in and out.

The circuit setup is similar to what we did in *Chapter 3, Blinking External LEDs* to blink external LEDs. At that time, we used P8_10 as the GPIO pin. Now we are connecting the LED to pin P9_21, which supports the PWM. You will need an LED, 470Ω resistor and a breadboard to set up this circuit. Power off the board and attach components to BeagleBone as shown in the diagram.

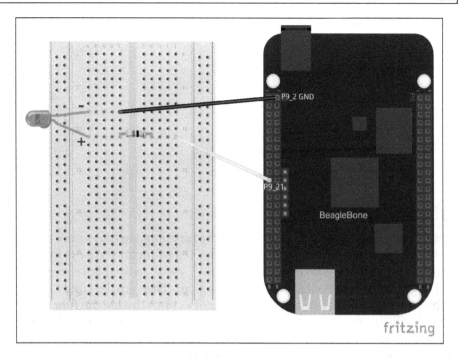

Program to fade in and fade out LED

Write the following code in Cloud9 and save it as `fadeLED.js`. Run the program and you should see the LED fading in and out alternatively.

The code for `fadeLED.js` is as follows:

```
var b = require('bonescript');
var led = "P9_21";
var loopTime = 20;
var duty_cycle=0;
var increment = true;

var loopTimer = setInterval(fadeLED, loopTime);

function fadeLED()
{
    if(duty_cycle == 100 )
        increment = false;
    if(duty_cycle == 0)
```

```
        increment = true;

    if(increment == true)
        duty_cycle = duty_cycle + 1;
    else
        duty_cycle = duty_cycle - 1;

    console.log("duty_cycle = ",duty_cycle/100);
    b.analogWrite(led,duty_cycle/100);
}
```

Explanation

In *Chapter 3, Blinking External LEDs* we used the function `digitalWrite()` with a similar setup. Here, we are using the `analogWrite()` function. We are initializing the variable `duty_cycle` with a value of zero. We use the variable `increment` as a Boolean flag to keep track of fading in or fading out. Then we declared `loopTimer` to call the `fadeLED()` function after each 20 milliseconds. Inside the function `fadeLED()`, we are checking the `duty_cycle` value. If it is equal to `100`, then we reached maximum limit. Here, we set the flag increment to `false` to mark that we will fade out now. If the `duty_cycle` is equal to `0`, we will mark the flag increment to `true`. Based on the flag value, we increment or decrement the duty cycle. Finally, we used the `analogWrite()` function to write a `duty_cycle` ratio on pin P9_21. This step actually puts PWM voltage on the pin.

In the beginning, the variable `duty_cycle` gets incremented by 1 after each 20 milliseconds from 0 to 100. Then it gets decremented by 1 after each 20 milliseconds from 100 to 0. When it is incrementing, the duty cycle of the PWM increases and so does the voltage on the pin. Increased voltage makes the LED brighter. When decrementing, the PWM duty cycle reduces the voltage on the pin. It makes the LED dimmer. This fade in and fade out happens alternatively till we stop the program. There could be errors related to device tree and sysfs file non-existence which go away after reboot. You can see device tree related messages using the `dmesg` command or in the `/var/log/messages` file.

If you shoot this LED with a high frame rate camera, you will see it is switching on and off. If you attach an oscilloscope to the pin, you will get a PWM waveform. The LED is not remaining ON for all the time. There are fluctuations. But they are fast enough (2 kHz) not to be captured by the human eye. Let's use the same technique to control a micro servo motor.

Micro servo motor circuit setup

We are going to control a micro servo motor. Servo motors are special types of DC motors tightly coupled with a feed-backing control circuit that positions a shaft in a precise angle. They are used where fast, accurate, and limited angle movement is needed, for example, robot arm movement and CNC machine. The position of the motor shaft can be controlled through PWM. There is no need for extra motor driver chip.

A micro servo motor can rotate 180 degrees. The frequency/period is specific as per the servo motor. A typical servo motor expects approximately a 20 millisecond period to drive the motor. A servo motor changes shaft angle as per pulse width. If the specified pulse width is 1 millisecond or less, it remains at angle zero. That translates to approximately 3% duty cycle. If the pulse width is 1.5 milliseconds, then the servo shaft will change to a 90 degree angle. If a 2 millisecond pulse is given, the servo shaft will be at a maximum 180 degrees. It translates to a 14.5% duty cycle approximately. So, if we want to drive the servo motor, we have to specify a duty cycle value between 3% and 14.5%.

For this exercise, we need a micro servo motor. Power off the board and attach the components to BeagleBone as shown in the diagram:

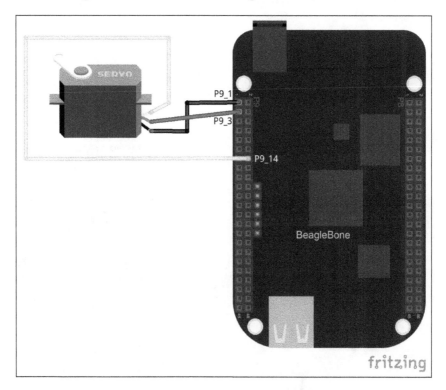

Program to control a micro servo motor

Write the following code in Cloud9 and save it as `microServo.js`. Run the program and you should see the servo motor moving from 0 to 180 degrees to and fro.

The code for is `microServo.js` as follows:

```
var b = require('bonescript');
var servo = 'P9_14';
var duty_min = 3;
var loopTime = 5;
var angle = 0;
var increment = true;

b.pinMode(servo, b.OUTPUT);
var loopTimer = setInterval(updateAngle, loopTime);

function updateAngle(x)
{

    if(angle == 180 )
        increment = false;
    if(angle == 0)
        increment = true;

    if(increment == true)
        angle = angle + 1;
    else
        angle = angle - 1;

        var duty_cycle = (angle * 0.064) + duty_min;
    console.log("angle =",angle);
    console.log("duty cycle = ",duty_cycle);
    b.analogWrite(servo, duty_cycle/100, 60);
}
```

Explanation

In this program, we created `loopTimer`, which will increment/decrement the shaft angle by one degree. We know that we have a limit of 3% to 14.5% to drive the servo. So, we created an equation where we get 180 values in the duty cycle range of 3 to 14.5:

```
duty_cycle = (angle * 0.064) + duty_min
```

where

`duty_min` = 3

`angle` = angle in between 0 to 180

Now, any value for the variable angle from 0 to 180 will give a `duty_cycle` value inside 3 to 14.5. We apply it using `analogWrite()`. We set the frequency to 60Hz, which creates a 16.66 millisecond pulse. This is near to the 20 millisecond period needed to drive the servo motor. The timer gets called after every 5 milliseconds and it calls the function `updateAngle()`, which either increments shaft angle by one degree or decrements by one degree. Inside `updateAngle()`, if the variable angle reaches the limits, that is, 0 or 180, then we toggle the flag variable `increment`. Based on this flag, we change the duty cycle inside range from 3% to 14.5% and then from 14.5% back to 3%. The servo shaft moves to and fro according to the duty cycle change.

Summary

In this chapter, we learned some theory about PWM. We saw that PWM is a way of creating analog values on digital pins. It can be used to drive analog output devices like motors, LEDs, speakers, and so on. We studied PWM waves and how a duty cycle can be used to control analog devices. BeagleBone has a special subsystem dedicated to generating PWM that work on subset of GPIO pins. Then we wrote a program to control the brightness of an LED via PWM. We also wrote a program to control the servo motor angle. Until now, we have done many physical computing exercises. Let's connect our BeagleBone to the Internet and control these physical components from the Internet. We will do this in next chapter. That will be our first step toward the **Internet of Things (IoT)**.

7
Internet of Things with BeagleBone

In the last chapter, we controlled analog components. We have done lots of physical computing exercises up to now. We used BeagleBone much like any microcontroller board doing electronics projects. But BeagleBone has many more capabilities. It has a full-fledged Linux operating system running inside it. It has an Ethernet port built-in. We have not used many of its capabilities yet. We can run it as a webserver and extend our physical computing programs to be executed from the Internet. In this chapter we will first learn about the Internet of Things. Then we will create a Node.js webserver running on BeagleBone and control a connected LED and servo motor remotely (even via smartphone). This will be our first step towards the Internet of Things. To cover a real-life example, we will program BeagleBone to e-mail when it detects overheating.

This chapter will cover the following topics:

- Why the Internet of Things?
- What is the Internet of Things?
- A program to create a new Node.js HTTP server
- A program to control an LED through the web browser
- A program to control a servo motor the through web browser
- Sending an alert e-mail on over-temperature
- What's next?

Why the Internet of Things?

The Internet of Things or IoT is a buzzword these days. Popular business analyst company Gartner has ranked *IoT* highest in the hype cycle of emerging technologies for 2014 and 2015. Analysts predict lots of growth in this technology. Many startups are working on this. Crowdfunding websites like Kickstarter (`https://www.kickstarter.com/`) and Indiegogo (`https://www.indiegogo.com/`) have successfully funded numerous IoT solutions. Established companies are investing a lot in IoT. Soon, we will see many of these *things* in our home and in our cities. Some of them are already available in the market, for example, smart bulbs that change their intensity depending on the outside light to save energy. They can also be controlled via smartphone app. The Amazon product *dash* can scan product barcodes or listen to any product name you say and that product is added to your Amazon online cart through your Wi-Fi connection. This saves time and effort when you want to buy multiple items. A wireless *pacemaker* helps control your heartbeat as well as store and provide heartbeat data logs wirelessly to decide medication. This was not possible previously without cutting into your skin. Our world will change a lot when we have connected smart watches, health bands, electrical plugs, room heaters, ovens, toys, door locks, helmets, street lights, parking lots, trash cans, coffee machines, and many more. So, it is important to know what we can do to implement IoT using BeagleBone.

We can see that technological growth has happened in different ages. A major milestone was achieved when the personal computer was invented. Soon many homes, institutes, and enterprises got access to computers. They were introduced to the digital world. People started using them for financial accounting, data backup, entertainment, publishing, and so on. The next age came along with the Internet. Homes with an Internet connection got connected. This communication solved lots of problems. People started exchanging information, creating social networks, hosting websites, using online banking, playing multiplayer games, using cloud backup, and so on. Still, connectivity was limited to the PC. It was often shared. There was no Internet connectivity option available for individuals all the time. The next era came along with smartphones. Anyone can remain online all the time using a personal smartphone. The average time individuals remain online has increased drastically. Social networks became even bigger after this. People started relying on information updates from institutes, employers, friends, and websites. People started making decisions based on the latest updates. Information is at everybody's fingertips.

When everybody is connected to the Internet, the next obvious era will be connecting every *thing* to the Internet, that is, the era of the Internet of Things. Communication in between these *things* to other things/humans will bring many possibilities. It will solve many problems. Smart things will exchange data to provide high availability of service, better interoperability, take safety measures, automation, gather data and analyze them, self-monitoring, notifying, and allowing the remote user to make decisions, and so on. IoT has diverse use cases in several industries like automobile, healthcare, agriculture, transportation, manufacturing and home automation, and so on. Humans have limitations. We cannot work 24 hours every day. We cannot remember all the data that we encounter. We do not like to do repetitive tasks. Here *things* come to rescue us. They can work 24/7 and can store and retrieve data on cloud storage accurately and reliably (considering a reliable network). Sensors and actuators give things the capability to know some information about the environment and respond. This information can be analyzed and visualized to draw important conclusions. IoT gives power to administer things remotely, which reduces distant visits including hazardous environment conditions.

What is the Internet of Things?

According to Wikipedia, IoT is a network of physical objects or things embedded with electronics, software, sensors, and connectivity. These things interoperate within the existing Internet infrastructure. They achieve greater value and service by exchanging data with the manufacturer, operator, and/or connected devices.

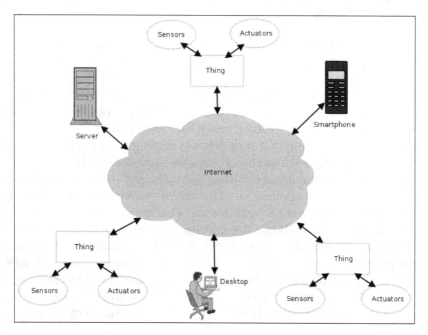

Properties of *things* involved in IoT:

- They are physical objects with input (sensors) and/or output (actuators). They interact with the physical world.

- They have connectivity to the Internet or local connectivity via Ethernet, Bluetooth, GSM, Wi-Fi, or any RF transreceiver.

- They exchange data with Internet websites or cloud or other *things*. Often this data is available to the end-user via smartphone, tablet, or PC.

- They have some kind of unique ID like IP address, RFID, or QR code.

- They do have small software logic that they follow. Once set up, almost no physical human interaction is involved.

- Set of interrelated things form a system, for example, a traffic control system gets formed by smart traffic cameras, smart road notice boards, servers that collect data from traffic cameras to display traffic information on smart road notice boards. IoT is a system of such systems.

You can think of IoT as a human body. There are five senses — light by eyes, sound by ears, touch by skin, smell by nose, and taste by tongue. Human actuators are sound generation by various parts of the mouth, movement of various body parts by muscles, various biochemical changes by controlling glands, and many more. The human body has a respiratory system, digestive system, muscular system, skeletal system, circulatory system. These systems exchange information with the centralized brain via nerves. A human body is a system of these systems. All these systems work together to achieve our living.

BeagleBone is a natural choice for the IoT developer. It is small in size. It has a built-in Ethernet port unlike regular microcontroller boards. The USB port on BeagleBone allows you to attach Wi-Fi, Bluetooth or any RF USB adapter to have that connectivity. It has lots of GPIO pins, analog control pins and buses to talk with sensors, and actuators. It needs less electrical power to operate than a regular PC. The BeagleBone CPU is powerful enough for lots of processing. It has a full-fledged Debian Linux running that supports lots of programming languages and many softwares including various server software. You can conduct moderate data processing, storage-retrieval using database software, and data analysis locally inside BeagleBone. There is no need for extra server machines for this. Kernel, bootloader, rootfs — all software is open source. That means software can be modified to individual needs. Even hardware design files are open source. Anybody can modify those to implement his/her custom IoT solution. All these benefits make BeagleBone the perfect candidate for IoT. With all this theory considered, let's move to write a few IoT programs using BeagleBone. IoT products can be classified based on scope into smart wearable, smart home, smart city, smart environment, smart enterprise. All the exercises in this book fall into the smart home category.

Program for creating new Node.js HTTP server

To control BeagleBone from the Internet we need to run an HTTP server on it. BeagleBone already has `Node.js` running as the HTTP server to be able to run Cloud9 on port `3000`. There are built-in `Node.js` HTTP interfaces that can be used to create a new HTTP server on a specified port number. Once created, this server listens to HTML queries on the specified port. On request, it sends an HTML file to the client. The client browser renders this HTML file. So, we have to write JavaScript code to run the `Node.js` HTTP server and write an HTML file to be displayed. Let's create a HTML file first.

HTML code

Open Cloud9 IDE and open a new file tab. Write the following code in it and save it as `iot.html`.

The code for `iot.html` is as follows:

```
<!DOCTYPE html>
<html>
<body>
  <h1>Beaglebone IoT</h1>
  <h2><a href="/led.html">LED</a></h2>
  <h2><a href="/servo.html">Servo</a></h2>
</body>
</html>
```

This is simple HTML code. This file can be viewed using the web browser. It has big header text— `Beaglebone IoT`. It has two links pointing to `led.html` and `servo.html` files, which do not exist yet. We will soon create them.

JavaScript code

Let's create the `Node.js` HTTP server. Write this program in Cloud9 and save as `baseHttpServer.js`. Run this program. It will run a new `Node.js` server on port number `3001`. Open the web browser from your laptop/computer/smartphone connected to the same router your BeagleBone is connected to. Put this address in the address bar: `http://<Beaglebone's ip address>:3001/iot.html`. We covered how to obtain BeagleBone's IP address in *Chapter 1*, *Cloud9 IDE*. Suppose BeagleBone's IP address is 192.168.7.2, then the address should be `http://192.168.7.2:3001/iot.html`. You should be able to see the text `Beaglebone IoT` in the browser.

The code for `baseHttpServer.js` file is as follows:

```
var http = require("http");
var fs = require('fs');
var url = require('url');
var port = 3001;

var myServer = http.createServer(httpRequestHandler);
myServer.listen(port);
function httpRequestHandler(request, response)
{
  var fullPath = '/var/lib/cloud9' +
    url.parse(request.url).pathname;
  console.log('fullPath: ', fullPath); //print file path
  fs.readFile(fullPath,fileReadHandler);
  function fileReadHandler(err, file)
  {
    if(err)
    {
      response.writeHeader(500);
      response.end('Error loading html file');
    }
    else
    {
      response.writeHeader(200);
      response.end(file);
    }
  }
}
```

Explanation

We are first including the HTTP module and naming it as `http`. We need it to create a new HTTP server. Similarly, we include an `fs` (filesystem) and `url` (uniform resource locator) module. They are needed to read HTML file and parsing URL. Then we called the `createServer()` method from the HTTP module. It returns a new instance of class `http.Server`. The function `createServer()` takes the parameter as the name of the `callback` function to be called on events. Here, the `httpRequestHandler()` function will be called when there will be any event triggered on the port it is listening on. Then we called the method `listen()` on port `3001`. In our case, if there is any event triggered on port `3001`, the function `httpRequestHandler()` will be called.

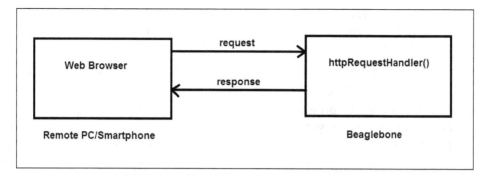

When `httpRequestHandler()` gets called, it is given parameters **request** object and **response** object. The request object has information about the HTTP request made to the server. The response is an object with fields that manages the response by the server. We read from the **request** object and fill the **response** object in `httpRequestHandler()`. This should be clear from the preceding image. First we crafted a full path of the HTML file to be sent to the client browser and printed the path for debugging. Make sure this path to the HTML file is— `/var/lib/cloud9/ iot.html`. Then we read the HTML file and after reading the `callback` function `fileReadHandler()` will be called with `err` and `file` as arguments. Inside the function `fileReadHandler()`, we check for errors. If there is an error, we modify the response object with the HTTP return code `500 error`. Then we called `response. end()`, which means the end response stream. If there is no error, we give the HTTP return code as `200 ok` and send our HTML file over the response stream.

Our experiment is limited to LAN. The browser from which you connect has to be inside LAN. If you want to allow connection to your BeagleBone from any system on the Internet, you can achieve it by using ngrok or any tunneling software. You can also achieve that for a specific port using the `port forwarding` option in your router's web configuration interface. In our case port `3001` has to be forwarded. DDNS service can help you to have persistent domain name for your BeagleBone. Please note this increases security risks.

Troubleshooting

1. It is recommended to use the Firefox or Chrome browser. They are available on Android and iOS as well.

2. Run command `netstat -nat | grep 3001` on the BeagleBone shell to confirm port `3001` is waiting for connection. You should get this output:

```
tcp        0      0 0.0.0.0:3001            0.0.0.0:*
LISTEN
```

3. Use `console.log()` frequently in our program to debug. It can be used to confirm control is reaching till the line. It can be used to print values of variables that you suspect might be troubling.

4. Some errors can be revealed from the client side. Use developer options in the browser to debug at the client side.

5. When you run this program multiple times, it may happen that `baseHttpServer.js` you ran earlier is still running. In that case, it causes a problem to start a new server on the same port. You will get `events.js:72 //unhandled exception`. You can find out the pid of older process instances using the command `ps aux | grep baseHttp`. Then you can kill it using the command `kill -15 <pid>`.

Program to control an LED through web browser

We have created a webserver on port `3001`. Now it is time to turn an external LED on and off using a HTML page remotely. Just by changing variable `ledPin` in the following JavaScript program to `USR0`, you can turn on/off onboard USER0 LED. This will save wiring efforts. We are going to use the JavaScript `socket.io` library for this. This library allows real-time, full-duplex, communication by sending and receiving events. Let's install it by running the following command in the BeagleBone shell.

```
sudo npm install -g socket.io
```

The npm is Node Package Manager. It is a package manager for JavaScript libraries. It works independent of the Debian package manager. The source code of `socket.io` is available here: `https://github.com/socketio/socket.io`.

HTML code

Let's create an HTML file first. Open Cloud9 IDE and create a new file named `led.html`. Write the following code in `led.html`:

```
<!DOCTYPE html>
<html>
<head>
    <script src="/socket.io/socket.io.js"></script>
    <script>
    var socket = io.connect();
    function ledOn()
    {
```

```
      socket.emit('ledPin', 'on');
    }
    function ledOff()
    {
      socket.emit('ledPin', 'off');
    }
    </script>
  </head>
  <body>
    <input type="button" name="ON" id="onButton" value="ON"
      onClick="ledOn();">
    <input type="button" name="OFF" id="offButton" value="OFF"
      onClick="ledOff();">
  </body>
</html>
```

Explanation

This HTML code is divided into two parts. One part is HTML code that creates two buttons named **ON** and **OFF**. When these buttons get clicked, they call the function ledOn() and ledOff() accordingly. This part is in the <body> tag. The second part is the JavaScript code inside the <head> tag. It uses socket.io library to talk with the server. This is client browser side scripting. The socket.io works by sending events like connect, message or disconnect. It allows you to emit custom events besides regular events. Here, we are emitting event named ledPin with data on when the **ON** button is clicked and data off when the **OFF** button is clicked. This sent event has to be handled on the server side.

JavaScript code

Now, let's write the server side code to turn the LED on/off based on events emitted. This code is addition to the previous baseHttpServer code. Create a new file in Cloud9 and copy-paste the previous baseHttpServer.js code as it is. Then append the following code and save it as IoTLED.js. You need to connect the LED to P8_10 pin as we did in the LED blinking exercise. Please refer to *Chapter 3, Blinking External LEDs* for a detailed image.

Run `IoTLED.js` inside Cloud9 and open `http://<Beaglebone's ip address>:3001/led.html` inside the browser on a smartphone/laptop/desktop. You will able to see two buttons **ON** and **OFF** in the browser. By clicking these buttons you should be able to turn the LED on and off. If it does not work, try the troubleshooting steps that we covered in the `baseHttpServer.js` program. You can replace the LED with a buzzer or relay. This will be useful in situations when you want to turn the buzzer on and off remotely. The relay can be replaced with an LED to give you the power to control AC devices inside the home.

```
var b = require('bonescript');
var ledPin = "P8_10";
b.pinMode(ledPin,b.OUTPUT);
var sockio = require('socket.io');
var io = sockio.listen(myServer);

io.sockets.on('connection', connectionHandler);
function connectionHandler(socket)
{
  console.log("Inside connectionHandler");
  socket.on('ledPin', ledPinHandler);
  function ledPinHandler(data)
  {
    console.log("data : " + data); //print received data
    if(data == 'off')
      b.digitalWrite(ledPin,b.LOW);
     else
      b.digitalWrite(ledPin,b.HIGH);
  }
}
```

Explanation

We took the old `baseHttpServer.js` code as it is. It created a new `Node.js` HTTP server. The additional code is for using `socket.io` and BoneScript. We included `socket.io` library code and named it as sockio. Then sockio started listening on our newly created server—`myServer`. We mapped the event connection to the callback function `connectionHandler()`. Now, when there is a connection event on the socket, the function `connectionHandler()` will be called. Inside the `connectionHandler()` function, we are waiting for event `ledPin`. If this event is emitted by the client side, it will execute a callback function `ledPinHandler()`. This function finally checks if the data emitted with event `ledPin` is coming from the **ON** button or **OFF** button in the `led.html` file. Based on data, it calls BoneScript's `digitalWrite()` to turn the LED on or off.

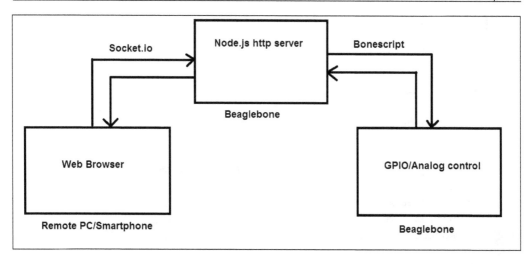

The whole communication can be seen in the preceding image. The Node.js server creates a new HTTP server and listens on port 3001. The remote web browser creates a connection with Node.js server using socket.io. It emits an event and data to the server. Based on the data, our server calls the bonescript function to control the electronic component. We avoided polling for data at the server side. The event-driven nature of JavaScript works efficiently here. Only required data is transmitted and received. In this exercise, there is one-way communication from browser to server to electronic component. But we can extend this to send data from the electronic sensor to the server and then from the server to the remote browser.

> IoT devices are connected all the time. So security becomes very important. A security bug can allow an attacker to take control of *things* remotely anywhere in the world. The security aspect of IoT is covered at the end of *Chapter 10, Internet of Things Using Python*.

Controlling a servo motor through LAN

We controlled an LED remotely. The same program can be extended to control a micro servo motor. But buttons inside the webpage cannot give real control on an analog motor. So, we will use a slider/range input to control the micro servo motor.

HTML code

Open Cloud9 IDE and create a new file named `servo.html`. Write the following code in `servo.html`.

The code for `servo.html` is as follows:

```
<!DOCTYPE html>
<html>
<head>
  <script src="/socket.io/socket.io.js"></script>
  <script>
    var socket = io.connect();
    function pwm(value){
      socket.emit('pwm',value);
    }
  </script>
</head>

<body>
  <div>
    <label for="servo">Servo:</label>
    <input type="range" name="servo" id="servo" value="50" min="0"
      max="180" onChange="pwm(value);">
  </div>
</body>
</html>
```

This HTML code is similar to the code from the `led.html` file. Here, we used range instead of buttons. Here, the range/slider can have a value from 0 to 180. When the range is changed, we call the function `pwm()` with slider value as the parameter. The function `pwm()` emits a `pwm` event with a slider value as data. This sent event has to be handled on the server side.

JavaScript code

Now, let's write server side code to move a shaft of the micro servo motor based on the slider value emitted. This code is in addition to the previous `baseHttpServer` code. Create a new file in Cloud9 and copy-paste the previous `baseHttpServer.js` code as it is. Then append the following code and save it as `IoTServo.js`. You need to connect a micro servo motor to P9_14 pin as we did in the micro servo motor exercise in the last chapter. Please refer to the last chapter for a detailed image.

Run this `IoTServo.js` inside Cloud9 and open `http://<Beaglebone's ip address>:3001/servo.html` inside the browser on a smartphone/laptop/desktop. You will be able to see the slider on the webpage inside the browser. When you move the slider to max position, the micro server rotates to 180 degrees. When you move the slider to the minimum position, the micro servo rotates back to 0 degrees.

```
var b = require('bonescript');

var sockio = require('socket.io');
var servo = "P9_14";
var duty_min = 3;

var io = sockio.listen(myServer);

io.sockets.on('connection', connectionHandler);
function connectionHandler(socket)
{
  console.log("Inside connectionHandler");
  socket.on('pwm', pwmHandler);
  function pwmHandler(angle)
  {
    console.log("angle = " + angle); //print received data
    b.analogWrite(servo, ((angle*0.064)+duty_min)/100, 60);
  }
}
```

You can combine `connectionHandler()` functions of both LED and servo code and get both HTML working in a single run. This program can be used to control a robotic arm remotely. The servo motor can be replaced with a DC motor to give you power to control the motor speed remotely.

Sending an e-mail on over-temperature

Suppose you want to maintain the temperature of the machine. If the temperature of the machine goes beyond 50 degree Celsius, you want to be notified by e-mail. This exercise can be part of your home automation. An Internet connection is essential for this exercise. Your router to which you connected BeagleBone should have some kind of working Internet connection via fiber, WAN port, DSL RJ11, or GSM dongle.

We are going to use the nodemailer JavaScript library for sending an e-mail using a Gmail account. Let's install it by running the following command in the BeagleBone shell:

```
sudo npm install -g nodemailer
```

The source code and other information can be found here: `https://github.com/nodemailer/nodemailer`.

We are going to use a Gmail account to send e-mail. Even a local mail server can be set up on BeagleBone to send e-mails. But it is a learning curve itself. Google does not allow you to e-mail directly using its SMTP servers. You need to use some settings in order for Gmail to allow you send e-mail via a program. Google provides two types of authentication for Gmail login:

1. Regular authentication: you just have to enter a username and password to log in. This is not considered to be a safe method. If you have not enabled two-step authentication, visit your Google security settings webpage: `https://myaccount.google.com/security` and turn on option **Allow less secure apps**.

2. Two factor authentication: You have to enter a username and password, as well as a six-digit code sent you by Google on your mobile. This is a much more secure way to access Gmail. If you have enabled two-step authentication, you will have to generate an app password for e-mailing via a program. Visit your Google security settings webpage—`https://myaccount.google.com/security` and click **App passwords** and generate a new app password for Mail on device Other. It will generate a 16-character password for you. You will have to use this new *app password* instead of your Gmail password in our program.

Create a setup the same as we did for temperature sensing using `tmp36` in *Chapter 5, Reading from Analog Components*. Open Cloud9 and write the following program and save it as `emailAlert.js`. Then replace the value of the variable `gmailFrom` with your Gmail ID and `gmailPasswd` with your Gmail password. Also, replace the value of variable `emailTo` to the e-mail address where you want to receive e-mails. This can be a Gmail address as well. Please note here you are saving your password in plaintext. There is a security risk. It is better to create a temporary Gmail ID and use it for this exercise.

```
var b = require('bonescript');
var nodemailer = require('nodemailer');

var threshold = 50;
var checkInterval = 4000;   //4 seconds
var gmailFrom = 'username@gmail.com'; //gmail address
var gmailPasswd = 'secretpasswd'; //gmail {app} password
var emailTo = 'username2@yahoo.com'; //email address where emails will
be sent
var temperature, volt;

var timer = setTimeout(readVoltageLoop, checkInterval);
```

```
function readVoltageLoop()
{
  b.analogRead('P9_40',checkOverTemerature);
}
function checkOverTemerature(pinObj)
{
  volt = pinObj.value * 1.8;
  temperature = (100 * volt ) - 50;   //Celsius
  console.log("Temperature = ",temperature.toPrecision(3));
if (temperature > threshold)
    {
      shootEmail();
      timer = setTimeout(readVoltageLoop, 3600000); // 1 hour wait
    }
    else
    {
      timer = setTimeout(readVoltageLoop, checkInterval);
    }
}
function shootEmail()
{
  var transporter = nodemailer.createTransport(
  {
    service: 'gmail',
    auth: {
      user:      gmailFrom,
      pass:      gmailPasswd
    }
  });
  var mailOptions =
  {
    from: 'Beaglebone <'+ gmailFrom + '>',  //sender
    to:    emailTo,  //receivers
    subject: 'Overtemperature alert!! : '+ temperature,  //Subject
    text: 'Current temperature : ' + temperature,  //plaintext
      body
    html: '<p>Current temperature : </p> <b>'+ temperature +
      '</b>'  //html body
  };

  transporter.sendMail(mailOptions, sentMailHandler);
  function sentMailHandler(error, info)
  {
    if(error)
```

```
        console.log(error);
     else
        console.log('Message sent' + info.response);
   }
 }
```

The `nodeMailer` variable has a preconfiguration for a Gmail SMTP service. We used it in our program to send e-mails. So, a Gmail account is needed for this exercise. But e-mails can be sent to any existing e-mail ID like `john@yahoo.com`. Once an e-mail is sent, you get a response like this from the Gmail SMTP server—`Message sent250 2.0.0 OK 1429777906 wa4sm7408653pab.17 - gsmtp`.

Explanation

This program includes `bonescript` and `nodemailer` libraries. Then we declared and initialized variables. We set a timer that will call callback the function `readVoltageLoop()` after 4 seconds. Inside the `readVoltageLoop()` function, there is a call to the `analogRead()` function, which reads the sensor voltage and the callback function `checkOverTemperature()` gets called. In this function, voltage is converted to degrees Celsius like we did in *Chapter 5, Reading from Analog Components*. Currently measured temperature is compared with threshold. If found to be greater, the function `shootEmail()` is called and then we wait for an hour before measuring voltage again. This is done to avoid sending too many e-mails in a short time. There is a limit to how many e-mails you can send in a day by Gmail.

Inside the `shootEmail()` function, we call the method `createTransport()` from the `nodemailer` library. We submitted the service provider (as Gmail), username and the password to this method. Then we filled `mailOptions` with information about the e-mail itself. The e-mail recipient, subject, and content are all decided here. Finally, we call the method `sendMail()` with the parameters `mailOptions` filled in earlier and callback the function name. Inside the `sendMailHandler()` callback function, we are printing an SMTP server response or error information if any.

You can visit the e-mail address specified in the variable `emailTo` and check if you got that e-mail. If not, check the spam e-mails folder as well. This program can be combined with the push-button program in *Chapter 4, Control LED by Push Button* to allow us to send an e-mail by button press.

Troubleshooting

1. If you get the error `getaddrinfo ENOTFOUND`, then it means there is a problem with internet connectivity.

2. If you get the error `Error: Invalid login code: 'EAUTH'`, then that indicates authentication was unsuccessful. Check your e-mail ID and app password.

3. If you get the error `cert_not_valid`, then that means mostly there is a problem with the date/time. Check the current time using the command `date`. Run command `ntpdate -b-s -u pool.ntp.org` to update the current time.

4. If the temperature threshold is not getting triggered, change the variable threshold to a low value like 25. You can increase the temperature by touching the sensor for some time.

What's next?

There are numerous JavaScript package modules available on `https://www.npmjs.com/`. Many of these packages provide APIs to do IoT fast and easy, for example, the `node-dropbox` module allows you to create, delete, and download files and folders on Dropbox. There are also modules related to various online services like Facebook, Twitter, Google-spreadsheet, and many more. You can do an interesting project combining our physical computing projects with them. There is a tool called Node-RED that allows you to create various IoT scenarios visually by a few mouse clicks. Installation and testing on BeagleBone is documented at: `http://nodered.org/docs/hardware/beagleboneblack.html`. Node-RED allows combining various hardware platforms, IO pins, network protocols, data formats, online services, and storage together in a visual way to create complex IoT scenarios. More details can be found at: `http://nodered.org/`.

We end our JavaScript programming part here. Before moving to another language there is a need to know what is yet left to do. We did not do any bus programming like I2C and SPI. We will cover that in the Python programming part. For now, the `bonescript` library does not have SPI implemented yet. It is work in progress. It might be implemented in near future. The source code of BoneScript can be downloaded from: `https://github.com/jadonk/bonescript`.

Summary

This chapter was about implementing IoT applications using BeagleBone. It combines physical computing exercises with Internet client/server programming. We first learned about the Internet of Things and its properties. Then we used the HTTP, `socket.io` and `bonescript` library at the server side to give client control of the LED and servo motor. At the client side, we wrote a small HTML + JavaScript code to display controls in the web browser. We created custom events at the client side and handled them in the server to respond. This gave us power to control the LED/servo remotely via our smartphone. We also programmed BeagleBone to shoot e-mail when it detects over-temperature using temperature sensor. This is the last chapter on the JavaScript part of the book. We will start coding in Python language in the next chapter with some physical computing exercises.

8
Physical Computing in Python

We used JavaScript language to program BeagleBone untill now. Now we'll focus on another popular language for programming BeagleBone — Python. It is a general purpose, widely adopted, high level language. It is easy to do coding in Python. Similar to BoneScript, there is a Python library from Adafruit that can do GPIO/Analog IO for BeagleBone. There is also an alternative library available called `PyBBIO`, which strongly follows the Arduino style of coding. As Adafruit's library is very similar to the BoneScript we learned earlier, we will follow it to code in Python throughout the book.

In this chapter, we will do many physical computing exercises in Python that we did in earlier chapters using `JavaScript/node.js`. It is assumed that you have gone through the earlier chapters. A good knowledge of the theory from *Chapter 2, Blinking Onboard LEDs* up to *Chapter 6, PWM – Writing Analog Information* is essential to get the most out of this chapter.

This chapter will cover:

- Python programming in BeagleBone
- Program to blink external LEDs
- Program to dance external LEDs
- Program to read from push button
- Program to print temperature
- Program to check light intensity
- Program to fade in and fade out an LED
- Program to control a micro servo motor

Python programming in BeagleBone

This is the first chapter of this book that talks about BeagleBone programming with Python. Let's get introduced to the Python language and compare it with JavaScript.

Python language is easy to code. Code written in Python is more readable than other languages. It is a high level language, which means the programmer does not have to worry much about hardware details while coding. A big program in low-level language can be replaced by a small program in Python with the same functionality. Python is a popular language and has a large community. You can find more resources on the official Python website at: `https://www.python.org/` and `https://docs.python.org/2/`.

There are some differences in JavaScript/Node.js and Python programming. Python is used in a wide range of applications besides the web. It follows synchronous execution. Unlike Node.js, Python is a blocking language. That means a Python interpreter waits until the current line execution completes before executing the next line. The sleeping function `sleep()` is available in the "time" library. There are many other differences. We will learn them eventually.

Adafruit BBIO library

Adafruit is an open source hardware company that sells electronic kits and parts. The official website is `https://www.adafruit.com/`. Most of the electronic components in this book are available on Adafruit. They have very good graphic tutorials available for kits, including BeagleBone. You can access them on: `https://learn.adafruit.com/category/beaglebone`. Besides this, they have written many open source applications and libraries for various kits. They have written a Python library to handle BeagleBone Input/Output. It is called `Adafruit_BBIO`. The source code for this library is available at: `https://github.com/adafruit/adafruit-beaglebone-io-python`. This library provides a set of Python tools to allow GPIO, Analog IO, I2C, and so on, access on BeagleBone. We are going to use it throughout the Python section.

This library comes pre-installed on the newer Debian distribution image available on beagleboard.org. You can check that by running the following command on the BeagleBone. Refer to *Chapter 1, Cloud9 IDE* to learn how you can get shell access on BeagleBone:

```
pip freeze | grep BBIO
```

This command should output something like `Adafruit-BBIO==0.0.20`. If it does not, you need to run the following commands to install it on Debian/Ubuntu on BeagleBone:

```
sudo ntpdate pool.ntp.org  ##sync time
sudo apt-get update
sudo apt-get install build-essential python-dev python-pip -y
sudo pip install Adafruit_BBIO
```

`pip` is a Python package manager just like `npm` for node. Alternatively, you can install the library manually from the GitHub source link given above.

Cloud9 IDE can also be used to do Python coding. It provides features like highlighting code, following indentation, and so on. But current version does not support debugging Python programs. To debug a Python program, you need to use the Python debugger `pdb` separately. The `pdb` is an interactive debugger similar to `gdb` debugger. We are not covering `pdb` in this book. Here is a link to a good tutorial to learn about using pdb: `http://pymotw.com/2/pdb`. In case of error, Python throws readable exceptions, for example. if you press *Ctrl + C* when the program is running, you will get a `KeyboardInterrupt` exception. Debugging readable exceptions is easier than errors in other languages. Alternatively, you can get shell access and use text editor like **vim**, and **emacs** to write Python programs instead of Cloud9.

 Please make sure you run programs with `sudo` privileges when running program from command line.

Program to blink external LEDs

Let's write LED blinking code in Python. Connect one external LED in series with a resistor to pin P8_10 like we did in *Chapter 3, Blinking External LEDs*. Type the following program in Cloud9, save it as `blink_external_LED.py` and run. You should be able to see an LED blinking each second:

The code for `blink_external_LED.py` is as follows:

```
#!/usr/bin/python
from time import sleep        ##Needed to call sleep()
import Adafruit_BBIO.GPIO as GPIO

led = "P8_10"

GPIO.setup(led,GPIO.OUT)

while True:
```

```
GPIO.output(led,GPIO.HIGH)
sleep(1)
GPIO.output(led,GPIO.LOW)
sleep(1)
```

Explanation

Now, let's go through the above-mentioned code snippet one step at a time. If you observed, there is no semicolon (;) at the end of lines in Python. There are no curly braces to indicate statements inside a `while` loop. Statements inside a loop are indented. Here is a line-by-line explanation of the code.

1. We declared that the interpreter of this program in `/usr/bin/python`. Now, you can change the permission of this file to executable and run directly in the shell. Shell will read the first line and execute it through the Python interpreter:

    ```
    sudo chmod  +x  /var/lib/cloud9/blink_external_LED.py

     /var/lib/cloud9/blink_external_LED.py
    ```

2. We imported the `sleep()` function from the `time` library. Comments in Python start with the symbol "#" similar to the shell program. Long multiline comments can be enclosed in triple apostrophes. For example `'''This is comment'''`

3. We included a GPIO namespace from the `Adafruit_BBIO` library and named it GPIO. This namespace has all the variables and functions related to GPIO. For detailed information about GPIO theory and GPIO pins on BeagleBone, please refer to *Chapter 3, Blinking External LEDs*.

4. We declared variable `led` and assigned it the value `P8_10`, GPIO pin `P8_10` is connected to our external LED. Now, we can access an actual LED via our `led` variable.

5. We called the function `GPIO.setup()`. This function is similar to the `pinMode()` function from BoneScript. The `GPIO.setup()` function sets the direction of the specified GPIO pin as `input` or `output`. As the LED is a component of "output" type, we set the direction as "output" for the pin. Now, we can write HIGH or LOW on the LED.

6. The `while` loop starts here. The condition for this loop is – `True`. "`while True:`" is equivalent to `while(1)` in C. This loop will run for ever. The number of indentations specifies which loop we are in. For statements inside a single loop, you use a single "tab" indentation. For statements inside a loop that is inside a single loop, you use a double "tab" indentation and so on. If you use the indentation incorrectly, the statement will be wrongly interpreted as part of another loop or you will get an indentation error.

7. Inside the loop we are calling the functions `GPIO.output()` and `sleep()`. The function `GPIO.output()` sets the LED pin `HIGH`, which glows the actual LED. Then the program sleeps for a second. After a second, it sets the LED pin `LOW`, which will turn off the actual LED. Then the program again sleeps for a second. This sequence runs for ever and we see the LED blinking for a second.

Program to dance external LEDs

In *Chapter 3, Blinking External LEDs* we did a dancing LEDs exercise. We created an illusion light is traveling from one end to the other and from the other end back. Let's write a Python program to achieve the same. Connect seven LEDs with resistors as shown in Chapter 3. Type the following program in Cloud9, save it as `dance_LEDs.py` and run. You should be able to see light travelling to and fro from both ends.

This is the code for `dance_LEDs.py`:

```python
#!/usr/bin/python
import Adafruit_BBIO.GPIO as GPIO
from time import sleep

LED_pins = ["P8_7","P8_9","P8_11","P8_13","P8_15","P8_17","P8_19"]

for led in LED_pins:
    GPIO.setup(led,GPIO.OUT)

while True:
    for led in LED_pins:
        GPIO.output(led,GPIO.HIGH)
        sleep(0.1)
        GPIO.output(led,GPIO.LOW)
    for led in reversed(LED_pins):
        GPIO.output(led,GPIO.HIGH)
        sleep(0.1)
        GPIO.output(led,GPIO.LOW)
```

Explanation

In this program, we have created a list of strings with the name LED_pins. This list has the name of all the GPIO pins that has actual LEDs connected to.

1. First, we iterated through this list and set the direction of all the pins as output.

2. Then we ran a while loop for ever. Inside the while loop, we used a for loop to iterate through the list LED_pins. Inside this loop, we turned each pin HIGH for 1 millisecond one by one. So, the actual LEDs glow one by one up to the other end.

3. After that, in another for loop, we did the same on reversed list of LED_pins. Python has the function reversed(), which reverses elements in a list. Here, we get actual LEDs glowing one by one in a reverse direction.

The above sequence runs until we stop the program manually. If you get any errors, please check the troubleshooting steps in *Chapter 3, Blinking External LEDs*.

Program to read from push button

In *Chapter 4, Controlling LED Using a Push Button*, we did a push button press detection exercise. Let's do the same in Python. Connect a push button as shown in Chapter 4. Type the following program in Cloud9, save it as push_button.py and run. You should get Button is pressed as the output when you press the button. When the button is not pressed, you get Button is released printed as the output:

```python
#!/usr/bin/python
import Adafruit_BBIO.GPIO as GPIO
from time import sleep
button = 'P8_16'

GPIO.setup(button,GPIO.IN)

while True:
    if GPIO.input(button) == True: # Checks if the pin is HIGH
        print("Button is pressed")
    else:
        print("Button is released")
    sleep(1)
```

Explanation

In the preceding code, we chose pin P8_16 to connect to the push button. The push button is a component of input type. So, we set the direction as input using the GPIO. setup() function. Now, we can read the state of the GPIO pin. As this is a digital component, the state will be HIGH or LOW. In Python, HIGH and LOW are mapped to Boolean True and False. The function GPIO.input() reads the state of the specified GPIO pin. If the actual button is pressed, it returns True otherwise it returns False. Inside the infinite loop, we check if the GPIO pin connected to the button is HIGH. If yes, Button is pressed is printed. Otherwise we print Button is released.

Detecting button state using interrupt

Our previous program prints the button state each second. Even if nobody presses the button for a long time, it will still wake up each second and check if the button is pressed. This is an inefficient polling mechanism. Also, if you press the button quickly in between two printings, it will be lost. A better approach to this problem is to use the "interrupt" mechanism. Let's write a program that uses the interrupt mechanism to detect change in the push button state. Type the following program in Cloud9, save it as push_button2.py and run it. You should get Button is pressed when you press the button. When you release the button, it will print Button is released.

```python
#!/usr/bin/python
import Adafruit_BBIO.GPIO as GPIO

button = 'P8_16'

GPIO.setup(button,GPIO.IN)

while True:
    GPIO.wait_for_edge(button, GPIO.RISING)
    print("Button is pressed")
    GPIO.wait_for_edge(button, GPIO.FALLING)
    print("Button is released")
```

Explanation

Let's see how the interrupt mechanism works. We set the direction of the GPIO pin P8_16 as the input. Adafruit BBIO library provides the function wait_for_edge() to register an interrupt. When the button is pressed, the voltage on pin goes from 0 to 3.3V. This is a voltage RISING event. When it is released, the voltage goes from 3.3 to 0V. This is a voltage FALLING event. An interrupt can be registered on the RISING event or FALLING event. When any of these events occur, the library is woken up and it continues execution of the program. When the actual push button is pressed, the CPU will get an interrupt of type FALLING. The interrupt handler will wake up the Python library, which will execute the next statement of printing Button is pressed. When the button is released, an interrupt of the type FALLING will be triggered. Control will reach to the next statement, which will print Button is released. Instead of printing, you can turn the LED on/off depending on the button pressed/released. This addition will achieve same result as of the program in *Program to control LED by push button* section from *Chapter 4, Controlling LED Using a Push Button*.

Program to print temperature

We learned about analog theory and BeagleBone's special analog input pins in *Chapter 5, Reading from Analog Sensors*. In that chapter, we read the temperature from the TMP36 sensor. Let's write a Python program to do the same.

Connect the TMP36 sensor to P9_40 as shown in the diagram in Chapter 5. Type the following program in Cloud9, save it as TMP36.py and run. It will print the current temperature in degrees Celsius. If you touch the sensor, you will see an increase in temperature.

This is the code for TMP36.py:

```
#!/usr/bin/python
import Adafruit_BBIO.ADC as ADC
from time import sleep

tmp36 = "P9_40"

ADC.setup()

while True:
    volts = ADC.read(tmp36)* 1.8
    ##Equation created after reading TMP36 datasheet
    temperature = (volts*100) - 50
    print "Current Temperature is " +
      str(round(temperature,2))
    sleep(1)
```

Explanation

This time we took the ADC namespace from the BBIO library. This namespace has variables and functions related to analog input. Function ADC.setup() initializes and tests analog entries in sysfs. Function ADC.read() reads analog voltage measured at the corresponding pin and normalizes it in a range of 0 to 1. We multiply it by 1.8 to get the actual voltage at the pin. Please refer to *Chapter 5, Reading from Analog Sensors* for details about the TMP36 sensor. The TMP36 datasheet gives us an equation to convert measured voltage to temperature in degrees Celsius. We used that equation to calculate the current temperature and printed it after rounding off using the function round(). You can use the LM35 temperature sensor instead. In that case you just need to change the equation line to temperature = (volts*100).

A Program to check light intensity

In *Chapter 5, Reading from Analog Sensors,* we used a **LDR (Light Dependent Resistor)** to measure light intensity. Let's write a Python program to do the same.

Connect the LDR to P9_38 as shown in the diagram in Chapter 5. It includes a voltage divider to reduce the high magnitude of output voltage. Type the following program in Cloud9, save it as LDR.py and run. It will print the output voltage. If the LDR is exposed to bright sunlight, you may get the output message – **Looks like a bright sunny day**. If this is not possible, point a torch on the LDR surface. You should see voltage has increased. In case it detects a high voltage, it will print that it is a sunny day.

```python
#!/usr/bin/python
import Adafruit_BBIO.ADC as ADC
from time import sleep

LDR = "P9_38"

ADC.setup()

while True:
    volts = ADC.read(LDR) * 1.8
    print "Voltage at input pin = " + str(volts)
    if (volts > 1.6):
        print "Looks like bright sunny day"
    sleep(1)
```

Explanation

This program has a similar logic to the last program. It does `ADC.setup()` to initialize and uses `ADC.read()` to read the voltage at pin `P9_38` in an infinite loop. Here, luminosity is directly proportional to voltage measured. Please refer to *Chapter 5*, *Reading from Analog Sensors*, for more details.

Program to fade in and fade out LED

In *Chapter 6*, *PWM – Writing Analog Information* we saw that to control analog devices, BeagleBone uses a PWM subsystem. It generates analog values on some specific pins turning that pin `HIGH` and `LOW` very fast in patterns. Learning PWM involved learning about frequency, period, duty cycle and average voltage in Chapter 6. The resultant voltage is proportional to the duty cycle. If the duty cycle is increased, the resultant voltage will increase. We generated a range of resultant analog voltage on pin by changing the duty cycle. We did a LED fade in and fade out exercise using PWM. Let's do that program again in Python.

Connect an LED to `P9_21` as shown in the diagram in Chapter 6. Type the following program in Cloud9, save it as `LED_fade.py` and run. You should be able to see the LED fading in and out for some time.

The following code is for `LED_fade.py`:

```python
#!/usr/bin/python
import Adafruit_BBIO.PWM as PWM
from time import sleep

led = "P9_21"

PWM.start(led)

for loop in range(0,10):
    for i in range(0, 100):
        PWM.set_duty_cycle(led, i)
        sleep(0.01)
    for i in range(0, 100):
        PWM.set_duty_cycle(led, 100-i)
        sleep(0.01)

PWM.stop(led)
PWM.cleanup()
```

Explanation

This time we took a PWM namespace from the `BBIO` library. This namespace has variables and functions related to the PWM output. The function `PWM.start()` loads the `am33_pwm` device tree and changes sysfs files according to the parameter provided to this function. The prototype of this function is `PWM.start(channel, duty=0.0, freq=2000, polarity=0)`. The parameter `channel` is the name of the pin on which you want to generate the PWM. Other parameters are optional. By default this function initializes the parameter duty 0, which means the duty cycle is zero and there will be no voltage generated on the pin. The frequency generated on the pin is 2,000 cycles per second by default. The parameter `polarity` is required to do advanced PWM configuration about rising or falling edge selection. Please refer to the Technical Reference Manual for more details on PWM.

Once the PWM is initialized on the pin, we can change the duty cycle and frequency run time. In order to fade in the LED, we used the function `set_duty_cycle()`. This function takes the name of the pin and the duty cycle value as parameters. Valid values of the duty cycle in the `BBIO` library are 0 to 100. We iterated from 0 to 100 and set that duty cycle after each millisecond. So we get the voltage on `P9_21` incrementing each millisecond. As a result, we see the attached LED fading in. Then we set the duty cycle from 100 to 0 decrementing after each millisecond. This results with the LED fading out.

Unlike the GPIO and ADC, it is important to de-initialize PWM. The function `stop()` does that. If it is not called, BeagleBone keeps on generating PWM on that pin. This function unloads the device tree from that particular channel and closes related sysfs files. Finally, the `cleanup()` function disables all exported PWM channels.

Program to control micro servo motor

Let's repeat another exercise from *Chapter 6, PWM – Writing Analog Information* to move a micro servo motor shaft to and fro. Connect the LED to `P9_14` as shown in the diagram in Chapter 6. Type the following program in Cloud9, save it as `microservo.py` and run. You should be able to see the motor shaft moving in 180 degrees to and fro:

```python
#!/usr/bin/python
import Adafruit_BBIO.PWM as PWM
from time import sleep

servo = "P9_14"
```

```
duty_min = 3

PWM.start(servo, 0, 60)

for loop in range(0, 10):
    for i in range(0, 180):
        ##move shaft from 0 to 180 degree
        PWM.set_duty_cycle(servo, (i*0.064) + duty_min)
        sleep(0.01)
    for i in range(0, 180):
        ##move shaft from 180 to 0 degree
        PWM.set_duty_cycle(servo, (180 - i)*0.064 + duty_min)
        sleep(0.01)

PWM.stop(servo)
PWM.cleanup()
```

Explanation

This program is similar to previous LED fade-in and -out program. As explained in *Chapter 6, PWM – Writing Analog Information,* the micro servo motor needs to be set at 60Hz. The duty cycle needs to be set from 3 to 14.5 in order to move shaft from 0 to 180 degree. So, we set 60 as frequency parameter in the PWM.start() function. Then we changed the duty cycle from 3 to 14.5 in 180 steps. This moves the shaft from 0 to 180 degrees. Then we reduced the duty cycle from 14.5 back to 3 in 180 steps. So, the shaft comes back to 0 degrees.

If you noticed, all the exercises work on different pin numbers. There is no common pin in any two exercises except the power and ground pin. That means we can have everything connected in all exercises and run all at a time on a single BeagleBone. The cover photo of this book gives an idea of how this would look like.

Summary

This chapter involved writing many Python programs that we did earlier in JavaScript/node. Python code is sequential and easy to understand. We used the `Adafruit_BBIO` library to do low-level input/output for BeagleBone. It provides the GPIO, ADC and PWM namespace with easy to use functions. We learned and used many such functions in programs in this chapter. This chapter covered all the physical computing exercises in Python that we did in JavaScript in the last few chapters.

The information we gathered up to now is sufficient to communicate with many input/output devices. Still, a few sensors/displays/components that use bus to communicate information cannot be interfaced with our current knowledge. We will see I2C, SPI and UART bus communication in the next chapter.

9

UART, I2C, and SPI Programming

In the previous chapter, we went through some Python examples on BeagleBone. We covered digital components and analog I/O devices. There are some sensors/devices that do not fit into these types. They accept or produce more data than traditional sensors/devices. Communication with them has to be done via an I/O bus. In this chapter, we will study a few popular I/O bus communication protocols in the embedded world and how they are supported on BeagleBone. Then we will program sensors/devices that support these protocols.

This chapter will cover:

- Bus and bus protocols
- What is UART?
- A program to read/write on UART
- I²C protocol
- Program to read from an ADXL345 sensor
- SPI protocol
- A program to write display text on the Nokia 5110 LCD

Bus and bus protocols

Up to now, we have dealt with digital and analog components. GPIO logic is much like ON/OFF switches. It is not good for exchanging complex information. Data exchange in between intelligent devices can not be done by GPIO logic. Then we dealt with sensors of analog type. Analog sensors generate voltage on output pin proportional to measured units. Reading information from them is straightforward. New generation digital sensors do a lot more than this. They accept and respond to supported commands. They can have the capability to do signal processing, data storage, analog-digital conversion, auto-calibration, and so on. They generate more information than digital HIGH/LOW or analog voltage equivalent to measured units. An example is GPS coordinates information by GPS sensor or current time information by the RTC clock. GPIO/analog logic is not enough to transfer this complex data. Besides these smart sensors, many output devices expect complex information for their work, for example, an LCD screen. So, there is a need for complex data transfer. The solution is to use the I/O bus.

In Wikipedia a bus is defined as a communication system that transfers data between components inside a computer, or between computers. A bus communication system involves physical interconnection lines between components/devices and software logic used for communication. One physical line is capable of transmitting signal representing one bit at a time. Physical interconnection in two components/devices can be done via multiple parallel data lines sending multiple bits at a time. It is called parallel bus, for example the old parallel port in a PC had eight parallel data lines. So it could transfer one byte at a time. Another physical interconnection way is to have a single physical line to transmit/receive data. It is called a serial bus. Here, one byte gets transferred when 8 bits are transmitted one after another on serial bus. This is time division multiplexing, actually. The advantage of a serial bus is that it minimizes the number of pins, lines and the size of the chip. Parallel buses lead to crosstalk and a time skewing problem when speed is increased. Therefore, many parallel standards have been dropped and serial standards have gradually been replacing them. Generic buses supported by BeagleBone are serial. So, this book only considers the serial bus. You need not to know detailed bus theory to do drive devices on these buses. You can skip theory section and jump to circuit diagrams and programs directly.

Bus logic for memory, GPU and other high-speed system bus components is out of the scope of this book. We will cover only bus logic for input/output peripherals. So the word "bus" is to be understood as "I/O bus" from now on.

I/O devices differ among themselves widely. Some devices respond very fast. Some devices are slow in response. Some devices generate a small amount of information to be read like an accelerometer. Some devices like webcams generate a continuously big amount of information to be read. If the same software logic applied to slow and fast devices, it would hamper the speed of fast devices and would exhaust slow devices. Also, some devices expect to know the transmission speed in advance. Others transmit according to clock signals. Overall, communication with different types of devices needs different sets of rules to be followed. These sets of rules are called bus protocols. Two components/devices must follow the same protocol in order for successful communication between them, for example a USB keyboard follows USB protocol. It has an internal chip that has USB protocol software logic. When a USB keyboard is connected to a USB port, the CPU starts using the USB device driver software logic. They both follow USB protocol logic and communication happens smoothly. Bus protocols can be used to exchange information between two systems as well, for example BeagleBone and Arduino can exchange information via UART serial bus protocol when connected correctly.

For a serial bus, it is ideal to have a dedicated line to transmit and receive data between every two components/devices that are communicating with each other. In this case, data transmission can happen at any time without signal overlap. Adoption of a new device becomes difficult here. But it is not practical to have separate physical lines in between all devices. So, bus standards support sharing of physical lines between multiple devices. This new change makes a bus easily expandable to new devices. Now, there are many devices sharing the same data line, which can start transmitting data at any time. If two devices transmit data at the same time on a shared data line, then the signal gets overlapped and data is lost. So, only one device should transmit at a time. There is the need for some governing entity here to decide which device can communicate at a given time. This problem is solved by making a single hardware device the bus controller or master. Any device on the bus that starts/stops transmission according to an instruction given by the master is called a slave. The master is like traffic police. It coordinates to make sure only one device is talking at a time. A slave never initiates communication. It responds only when addressed.

For successful data transmission, there should be time coordination between the transmitter and receiver. The receiver can see only changes in signal over the time period. There should be some way for the receiver to detect individual bits from this, for example if the data line was kept HIGH for 10 milliseconds by transmitter, it is not clear if that means five bits 11111 or 10 bits 1111111111 data or it could be anything else. To solve this problem, an extra physical line for a clock signal is introduced to have all data transfer events synchronized. The clock line is shared among all devices on the bus. All the devices on the bus can read the clock line and all events start at the beginning of the clock cycle. The clock signal provides a reference signal for devices to use when exchanging data. Often, one bit of data is transferred with each clock cycle. Now, if the physical line is kept HIGH for 10 milliseconds and 5 clock cycles are completed in 10 milliseconds on the clock line, then the receiver will interpret data as five bits – 11111. The bus protocol using this solution is called synchronous bus. Another solution is to have special "start" and "stop" bits for synchronization along with each data byte. The "start" bit alerts the receiver that a new byte is coming. Internal timing units are adjusted accordingly after each byte transfer. So, even if the transmitter or receiver clock source crystal has a small time deviation, the receiver does not get out of alignment with the transmitter. The timing unit in communicating devices is still independent here. There is no common clock reference signal for synchronization. So, this type of bus solution is called an asynchronous bus. Asynchronous communication has an overhead of "start" and "stop" bits with each byte transfer. But it saves extra clock lines and pins.

There are many standard bus protocols. Most devices/sensors follow one of the standard bus protocols. The BeagleBone processor has some pins that support interfacing with popular bus devices, for example I2C, SPI, CAN and UART devices. We will cover UART, I2C and SPI in this chapter. We will need the above theory about bus to study the characteristics of these buses.

What is UART?

Universal Asynchronous Receiver Transmitter (UART) is a simple and popular way of serial communication. UART is used to convert data bytes on a parallel bus to serial bit stream which can be sent on a communication line. If this bit stream is given to another UART, it can convert back to the original data bytes. UART uses asynchronous communication, which means it follows all the asynchronous bus rules we learned in the previous section. It also uses optional error checking methods. It was actually a serial chip inside a PC motherboard or serial devices inside a modem, serial mouse, and so on. This IC implements a basic serial communications protocol that transmits and receives up to eight data bits at a time. Over time, UART logic has become widely adopted by embedded systems to give a user system log and console access. Even BeagleBone has serial pins near the P9 header to get system log and console access. Many microprocessors/microcontrollers and electronic devices have UART logic integrated for serial communication. UART is a simple and popular way of serial communication. There are well known Wi-Fi, Bluetooth, RFID modules and GSM modems that support UART communication.

UART standard is all about how data is transferred from one place to another. It does not specify physical parameters like logic level, signal timing, transmission medium, and mechanical connectors. There are different physical standards that can be used with UART like RS-232 and RS-485. They often require a logic level convertor chip. These standards guarantee transfer speed based on distance. Using a standard for physical implementation is convention not compulsion. It is possible to do serial communication between two UART devices at the processor's default logic level (3.3V for BeagleBone) without using any level convertor. This is a simple physical implementation of UART without a standard. There is no throughput guarantee. But this communication works fine if the cable is not very long. Many embedded systems including BeagleBone and devices with a UART bus follow this approach.

In UART, data format and transmission speed are configurable. That is why it has the word "universal" in its title. In data format, the user can configure 5–8 bits of data. The optional single bit of parity can be even or odd. The stop bit can be 1 or 2. By default the data format remains 8N1 which means 8 bit data, no parity bit and 1 stop bit. Transmission speed is configured in the unit baud rate. The baud rate is the number of signal state changes per second. Based on the modulation technique, one baud may represent one or more bits. UART is usually configured with the standard baud rate numbers 9600, 19200, 38400, 57600, 115200. Data format and baud rate configuration must match for both transmitter and receiver in order to have successful communication. There are many variants of UART connection. The simplest UART port just uses **TX** (transmit) and **RX** (receive) pins. Two-way full duplex communication is possible by connecting the RX pin of the transmitting system/device to the TX pin of the receiving system/device.

UART is one-to-one communication. It also means if you want to connect many UART devices to BeagleBone, you will need the same number of UART ports on BeagleBone. The BeagleBone processor has a maximum of six UART connections possible. The UART0 port is dedicated to give kernel log and console access to the BeagleBone user. There are six male pins located near the P9 header. UART3 has a TX pin but no RX pin. So, it can be used only to send information from BeagleBone to the connected device. UART4 and UART5 share the same pin that HDMI is using. So, if you want to use UART4 or UART5 then you will have to disable HDMI. This is covered in the *Appendix C, Pinmux and Device Tree*.

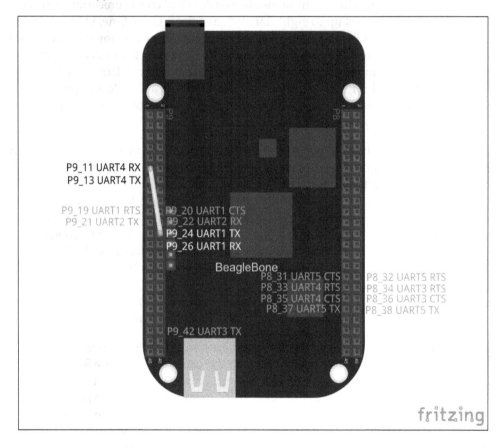

After learning theory about UART, we are ready to write our UART read/write program. Check the above diagram to learn about the UART pins on BeagleBone as well as how to do the connection for our next program. Pins with faded grey text are not enabled by default. Please refer to the *Appendix C, Pinmux and Device Tree* for information on how to enable them. Usually, UART1 and UART4 are enabled by default. There are some RTS (Request To Send) and CTS (Clear To Send) pins. These pins are helper pins and are optional. As a programmer, there is no need to know much of protocol implementation. Once connected, whatever is written on one UART port is available to read on the UART of the other end. If we connect the TX pin of the UART1 port to the RX pin of UART4 then whatever is written on UART1 is available to read on UART4. We will test write code on the UART1 port and read code on UART4. This is not a two-way full duplex connection. But it is sufficient to cover reading and writing on the UART device we want to test. If we connect P9_13 pin to P9_26 pin, there will be a two-way connection between UART1 and UART4.

Program to read/write on UART

UART implementation inside the Adafruit Python library has methods to set up and start UART channels, load an appropriate device tree and to clean up. It does not provide actual UART read/write methods as they are already part of the Python module "pyserial." There is a need for a "pyserial" Python module installation to read/write on the UART channel. Run the following command:

```
sudo pip install pyserial
```

Connect pin "P9_24" (TX pin of UART1) to "P9_11" (RX pin of UART4) using a jumper wire. Type the following two programs in Cloud9, save them as UART1. py and UART4.py. Run UART4.py first. Then run UART1.py. You should see Hello World printed on the output window of program UART4.py.

This the code for UART1.py:

```
#!/usr/bin/python

import Adafruit_BBIO.UART as UART
import serial
import time

port = "/dev/ttyO1"
baudrate = 9600
write_str = "Hello World\n"

UART.setup("UART1")
```

```
ser1 = serial.Serial(port, baudrate)
ser1.close()
ser1.open()
if ser1.isOpen():
    print("Serial is open")
    ser1.write(write_str)
    time.sleep(1)
ser1.close()
```

This the code for UART4.py:

```
#!/usr/bin/python

import Adafruit_BBIO.UART as UART
import serial
import time

port = "/dev/ttyO4"
baudrate = 9600

UART.setup("UART4")

ser4 = serial.Serial(port, baudrate)
ser4.close()
ser4.open()

if ser4.isOpen():
    print("Serial is open")
    read_str = ser4.readline()
    print(read_str)
    time.sleep(1)
ser4.close()
```

Explanation

Both programs are very similar. UART1.py is writing on serial port UART1 and UART4.py is reading on port UART4. Both import the UART part of Adafruit_BBIO Python library and the serial module we installed. Both programs call the UART.setup() method on the respective UART port to initialize them. Here, the device tree for that UART is loaded, and the corresponding UART channel is exported. The BBIO library creates new device entries /dev/ttyO1 (associated with UART1 port) and /dev/ttyO4 (associated with UART4 port). Then we created two connection objects **ser1** mapped to port **/dev/ttyO1** for writing string and **ser4** mapped to port **/dev/ttyO4** for reading string. Both objects are configured with the same 9600 baud rate. Later, both connections are closed first and then opened to avoid reopening of the UART device which is opened already by another process. UART4.py ran first and called the method **readline()** on UART4. So, the RX pin of UART4 (P9_11) started waiting for data. UART1.py ran later and wrote the string "Hello World\n" on UART1. So, the TX pin of UART1 (P9_24) started transmitting the string. As we connected the Tx pin of UART1 is connected to the Rx pin of UART4, the transmitted string was received at UART4. The method **readline()** in UART4.py got the string. This string has a line ending character "\n." So, the **readline()** method returns. The received string is printed by UART4.py. Both programs called the method **close()** on the connection object. The method **readline()** can be replaced with the method read(number_of_bytes) if you wish to wait for a certain number of bytes instead of "\n."

Troubleshooting

1. Try running outside of Cloud9. Sometimes the output of programs get mixed up in output windows in Cloud9. You can run a Python program directly in the BeagleBone console.

   ```
   sudo python /var/lib/cloud9/UART1.py
   ```

2. Note that the character in ttyO1 is not zero but the letter "O".

3. This program should be calling the function UART.cleanup() at the end for cleaning up sysfs entries. But the UART.cleanup() method causes kernel panic when unloading the device tree. This is a known kernel bug that comes with the current Debian image. A workaround is not to call it or restart BeagleBone. So, we skipped calling this method at the end.

BeagleBone Green comes with an onboard UART and I2C grove connector. You can attach many compatible UART and I2C grove modules directly to these connectors. This reduces prototyping work. You can get BeagleBone Green compatible modules. A list is available on this page: http://www.seeed.cc/beaglebone_green/.

I2C protocol

Inter Integrated Circuit (IIC or I²C or I2C) is a serial bus invented by Philips (now NXP). It is popular in the embedded world to interface low speed sensors/devices. It is implemented in more than 1,000 different ICs manufactured by more than 50 different companies. Popular I2C devices include Real Time Clock (RTC), EEPROM ICs, LCD/LED screen display, DAC, ADC, I/O expanders. There are many sensors that support I2C connection like temperature, pressure, humidity, accelerometer, digital compass, and so on. Many I2C bus variants are widely used in consumer electronics, for example System Management Bus (SMBus) is used on computer motherboards for communication with the power source and temperature/voltage/fan sensors. Display Data Channel (DDC) allows the monitor or display to inform the host about its identity and capabilities. I2C specifications are available at this link: `http://www.nxp.com/documents/user_manual/UM10204.pdf`

I2C bus protocol allows exchange of data through a single data line and clock line. A clock line is called SCL (Serial Clock) and a data line is called SDA (Serial Data). As a clock signal is shared over a clock line, communication is synchronous. Data transfer is bi-directional on single data line. I2C has various modes that work at different speeds from 100 kbits/s to 3.4 Mbits/s. Multiple devices can be connected to single bus. Still, physical interconnection complexity is not there because of only two lines connection. The master device on the bus provides a clock on SCL. It initiates transfer by generating a start and stop condition. It allows a specific slave to talk. It also determines data transfer direction. Every I2C slave device has a 7-bit or 10-bit identification/address. It is usually preconfigured by the manufacturer and listed in the datasheet. Several slaves can be there in the bus. But they should have different IDs. The master uses these IDs to select specific slave device for communication. A I2C bus can have multiple masters. When the stop condition is detected all compete to arbitrate the bus. Whoever succeeds controls data transfer until the next stop condition.

I2C has a major advantage over other buses in that two lines are enough to connect many sensors/devices (there is a need for Vcc and GND connection as well for a device to operate). This reduces the size of the chip, interconnection on PCB and the overall cost of the system. Prototyping is very easy for I2C connection. It has modes that can transfer data faster than UART standard speed numbers. There are some disadvantages as well. Only one device at a time can talk with the master on the bus. It can lead to the starvation of other devices. I2C data transfer is half duplex which is slow when data is getting transferred two ways at the same time. The I2C bus works fine over small distances only. An increase in cable length starts creating a problem. You cannot connect high-speed devices to I2C. I2C is suitable to connect low speed sensors/devices only. Each sensor/device needs to store I2C ID/address. Devices can have address conflicts. Some device manufacturers allow the selection of an address from a small range to overcome this problem.

BeagleBone has three I2C bus channels (I2C0, I2C1, I2C2), of which I2C0 is not populated and used internally to communicate with HDMI, EEPROM, power mgmt chip. I2C1 is disabled by default. Only I2C2 is available for communication by default. I2C hubs can increase the number of free I2C ports. When sensors/devices are connected to I2C pins on BeagleBone, it works as the master. In our next exercise, we are going to connect the ADXL345 accelerometer module via the I2C bus. ADXL345 is a small, low power, high resolution (13 bit) triple-axis accelerometer. It measures gravity acceleration useful in tilt-sensing applications. It is a micro electro-mechanical device that measures change in capacitance of the plates with polysilicon springs. More information can be found at: http://www.analog.com/en/products/mems/mems-accelerometers/adxl345.html.

Refer to the following diagram to get information about the I2C pins available on BeagleBone as well as how to connect ADXL345.

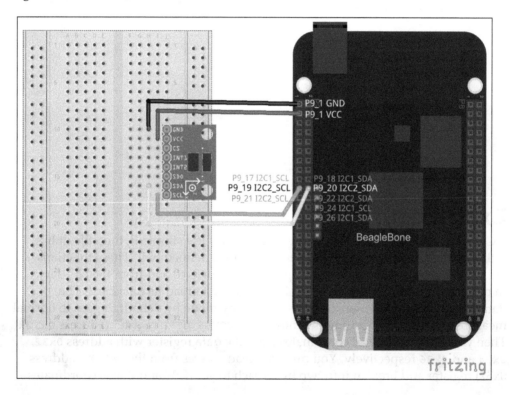

 Please note that this is a ADXL345 module with pull up resistors that exist on PCB. If it is a simple breakout board without a pull-up resistor, then you will have to add a 5K–10K resistor between the power pin and the SCL and SDL pins. It is recommended that you buy a module rather than breakout board.

Program to read from ADXL345 sensor

Connect the ADXL345 module to BeagleBone as shown in the diagram. Type the following program in Cloud9, save it as ADXL345.py and run it. You should see a three-axis coordinates list printed after every 2 seconds. If you move the sensor, you will see a change in coordinates.

```
from Adafruit_I2C import Adafruit_I2C
import time

ADXL345_I2C_ID            = 0x53 # I2C bus id
ADXL345_REG_POWER_CTL     = 0x2D # Power-saving control
ADXL345_REG_DATAX0        = 0x32 # X-axis data 0

accel = Adafruit_I2C(ADXL345_I2C_ID,debug=False)
accel.write8(ADXL345_REG_POWER_CTL, 0x08)

while True:
    raw = accel.readList(ADXL345_REG_DATAX0, 6)
    result = []
    for i in range(0, 6, 2):
        g = raw[i] | (raw[i+1] << 8)
        if g > 32767: g -= 65536
        result.append(g)
    print "result = " + str(result)
    time.sleep(2)
```

Explanation

I2C implementation in the Adafruit_BBIO library is a simple Python file. It has a class named Adafruit_I2C and a few functions defined in it. These functions are mostly about reading and writing in bytes/words to and from the I2C device. In order to communicate with ADXL345, we need to read its datasheet. The datasheet states that the sensor starts in standby mode by default. It goes to normal measurement mode by setting the third bit in POWER_CTRL register (address 0x2D). Then you can read X, Y, Z coordinates from the data register with address 0x32, 0x34 and 0x36 respectively. You can even read 6 bytes from the DATAX (address 0x32) register and break it into two bytes each to get X, Y, and Z axis coordinates.

In our program, we first called constructor Adafruit_I2C() with the parameter "0x53" which is the I2C address of ADXL345. Then we wrote 0x8 on the POWER_CTRL register of the sensor, which also means we set the third bit of the register to get it out of standby mode. We read 6 bytes starting from the DATAX register using function **readList()**. Then we copied 2 bytes into a single element of the **result** list in a loop and printed it.

Troubleshooting

- Linux provides excellent tools for I2C device communication under package "i2c-tools." ADXL345 has the I2C address `0x53`. When you connect it to BeagleBone, run the following command on the BeagleBone shell. This command shows the addresses of all I2C devices connected to the I2C2 bus of BeagleBone. Confirm that the fifth row and third column have the value "53."

  ```
  i2cdetect -y -r 1
  ```

- You can turn on debugging by providing the parameter "`debug=True`" to the constructor Adafruit_I2C().

- ADXL345 supports both I2C and SPI modes. Only one mode can be active at a time. Most of the time, the I2C mode is enabled by default. If you cannot see it detected using the "`i2cdetect`" command above, attach the CS pin of ADXL345 to 3.3V.

SPI protocol

The I2C bus interface is used for low-speed devices only. If you want to communicate with faster devices like LCD/LED display units, SD cards, Ethernet modules, then you need to use a faster bus on BeagleBone called the **Serial Peripheral Interface** (**SPI**). It provides high data rates in MB/s. Many sensors, DAC, Wi-Fi boards, and microcontroller boards support the SPI protocol. This protocol was developed by Motorola. It is popular in embedded systems.

SPI is a synchronous serial 4-wire protocol. Multiple devices can be connected to a single bus. So, it is a master-slave bus. One line is used to synchronize the clock signal (SCK/SCLK/CLK). The master provides the clock signal to all slaves. Two lines of MOSI and MISO are used to exchange data. MOSI carries data from the master to slave. MISO carries data from the slave to the master. So, SPI is a full duplex communication. MOSI and MISO lines are shared among all slave devices. One line is Chip Select (CS). It is also called Chip Enable (CE). The CS line is not shared. There is a separate line for each master-slave CS connection. So, the master needs as many CS pins as there are slaves to be connected. If not, regular GPIO pins can be used as a CS pin. It is active low which means if it is made LOW, that slave can communicate with the master. The master selects one slave among many on the bus for communication by changing the value on the CS pin. Once selected, communication happens only between that slave and master. The SPI protocol does not specify speed, flow control or any communication details. Different vendors expect different parameters. This gives protocol flexibility to manufacturers. SPI has the advantage of speed over I2C and UART. SPI speed is often more than 10 MBit/s.

The major disadvantage of SPI is—as slave devices on a bus increase, the number of connections increase. It becomes difficult to connect multiple devices. Also, there is no way to detect devices on a bus like I2C has. SPI works over short distances only compared with some UART standards. Some devices like a webcam need even more speed for communication. They can be interfaced with the USB port on BeagleBone.

BeagleBone has two SPI bus channels – SPI0 and SPI1. BeagleBone Black uses some pins of SPI1 for HDMI connection. So, you need to disable HDMI if you want to use the SPI1 bus. Refer to the following diagram to get information about SPI pins available on the BeagleBone:

Let's write a program to interface the Nokia 5110 graphic LCD display using the SPI0 bus on BeagleBone. This was part of the Nokia 5110 handset. But it is still widely available in the embedded market. It uses a Philips PCD8544 controller chip inside. It can drive a black and white graphic display of 48x84 pixels. It has all SPI pins except a MISO pin as it is an output-only device. There are additional pins like Reset (RST/RES), LED control, and data/command pin (DC). The MOSI pin is sometimes labelled as DIN or SDIN:

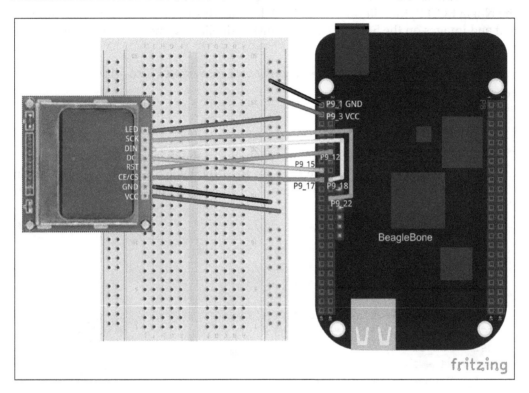

Program to write display text on Nokia 5110 LCD

Before running any SPI based program, we need to enable the SPI pins. There is a need to load a device tree overlay related to SPI from /lib/firmware. Run the following command as the root in the BeagleBone console:

```
ls /lib/firmware | grep -i SPI
```

This command should output something like "ADAFRUIT-SPI0-00A0.dtbo" and "ADAFRUIT-SPI1-00A0.dtbo" on the terminal. Then run the following command. The change string is getting echoed in the following command according to the output of the previous command.

```
sudo sh -c "echo ADAFRUIT-SPI0 > /sys/devices/bone_capemgr.8/slots"
```

Writing about all the LCD logic drivers is out of the scope of this book. Let us use the Nokia LCD Python library made by Adafruit. This library has a driver to draw text and images on the 5110 LCD. Let us install the library and its dependency module pillow:

```
git clone https://github.com/adafruit/Adafruit_Nokia_LCD.git
cd Adafruit_Nokia_LCD
sudo python setup.py install

sudo pip install pillow
```

Connect Nokia 5110 LCD to BeagleBone as shown in the diagram. If you cannot see LEDs on the display lit, connect the LED pin to GND. Type the following program in Cloud9, save it as Nokia5110.py and run. You should see the text "Hello World" on the LCD display:

```python
import math,time
from PIL import Image, ImageFont, ImageDraw
import Adafruit_Nokia_LCD as LCD
import Adafruit_GPIO.SPI as SPI

# Beaglebone Black hardware SPI config:
DC = 'P9_15'
RST = 'P9_12'
SPI_PORT = 1
SPI_DEVICE = 0 text = 'Hello World'

disp = LCD.PCD8544(DC, RST, spi=SPI.SpiDev(SPI_PORT, SPI_DEVICE, max_
speed_hz=4000000))
disp.begin(contrast=60)
disp.clear()
disp.display()
image = Image.new('1', (LCD.LCDWIDTH, LCD.LCDHEIGHT))
font = ImageFont.load_default()
draw = ImageDraw.Draw(image)

print 'Press Ctrl-C to quit.'
while True:
        draw.rectangle((0,0,83,47), outline=255, fill=255)
```

```
x=0
for c in text:
        x = x + 7
        draw.text((x,0),c,font=font,fill=0)
disp.image(image)
disp.display()
time.sleep(0.1)
```

Explanation

This program gives BeagleBone the ability to display any text on the LCD display. Ultimately we are creating a rectangle image of pixel size 47x83 with our text inside and then displaying it on screen. The same program can be used to display the output of our previous programs that we were printing on the console, for example printing temperature and accelerometer value on LCD.

We are making use of the `Adafruit_Nokia_LCD` library. When you download this library using Git in the above steps, you get source code available on BeagleBone. The LCD interfacing code is available in file `PCD8544.py` inside the source code. This file calls the `spi.BitBang()` and `spi.write()` functions from the `Adafruit_BBIO` library internally to send data to LCD via the SPI protocol at the time of initialization and when the function `display()` is getting called.

Summary

This was a long chapter with lots of theory and examples about buses on BeagleBone. We learned first that a bus is an interconnection of lines with software logic for data transfer. Different sensors/devices follow different set of rules for connection called bus protocols. The BeagleBone processor has support for UART devices and I2C, SPI buses. All these are serial protocols. We learned that UART is one-to-one connection carrying out asynchronous data transfer. Then we learned about the I2C and SPI bus. We wrote programs to read/write from UART, read from the ADXl345 sensor via I2C and displayed text on the Nokia LCD via SPI. We covered major buses supported by BeagleBone. Now, we will move to writing IoT programs in Python in the next chapter.

10
Internet of Things using Python

In the last chapter, we learned about different buses supported on BeagleBone. In this chapter we are going to take our physical computing exercises to the next level. In this chapter we are doing similar **Internet of Things** (**IoT**) exercises in Python that we did in *Chapter 7, Internet of Things with BeagleBone*. However, we will go one step further to upload and visualize our sensor data on the remote cloud. All our programs will be done using the Flask web framework. We will also implement a web app using the popular *REST*. The theory about the IoT is covered in Chapter 7. So, we will move to the programs directly. We will also cover security and other aspects in the last part of this chapter.

This chapter will cover:

- Flask web application framework
- Program to display temperature remotely
- Program to control an LED through a web browser
- RESTful web app to control a servo motor
- Program to trigger an e-mail alert on over-temperature
- Upload sensor data on cloud and visualize – ThingSpeak
- What's next?
- Security

Flask web application framework

We used the node.js framework to write IoT programs in Chapter 7. Let's create web applications in Python similar to what we did in Chapter 7. There are many HTTP frameworks available in Python. Most popular Python web application frameworks follow **Model-View-Controller** (**MVC**) design for coding, for example Django, and web2py. This design itself is a learning curve. So, we will skip them and choose another popular web framework that does not enforce MVC. **Flask** is an open source, lightweight web application framework for Python. Web applications can be written quickly in a single file. The *Hello World* program written on the Flask website homepage (which prints **Hello World** in the web browser) is just seven lines long. Flask web apps are more lightweight than MVC, which is good for embedded systems. Flask follows **Web Server Gateway Interface** (**WSGI**) specifications, which helps to create portable web applications. Many interesting web applications are written in Flask. For example, **Flaskr** is a blogging application:

```
http://github.com/mitsuhiko/flask/tree/master/examples/flaskr
```

Minitwit is a twitter clone:

```
https://github.com/mitsuhiko/flask/tree/master/examples/minitwit/
```

The following is a list of known websites that are running on Flask:

```
http://flask.pocoo.org/community/poweredby
```

Let us install it on BeagleBone.

Installation

Installing Flask is easy. Run the following command in the BeagleBone shell:

```
sudo pip install flask
```

This command installs Flask and all dependencies that are needed. Then you can import the Flask module and use functionalities provided by it in any Python program. Now that we have Flask up and running, let's write first a program to display temperature in a web browser remotely.

A program to display temperature remotely

This is a useful program in real-life and can be part of your home automation. You will be able to get temperature information from BeagleBone to any Internet connected smartphone/computer. We need to create one HTML file and one Python file for this exercise. Let's write an HTML file first. This HTML file is not hard-coded to show temperature value. It will get temperature value at run time. This type of HTML file defines a pattern or model of how a webpage should look at run time. So, they are called *templates* in Flask. A template HTML file needs to be created inside the directory *templates*. So, open Cloud9 IDE. Inside the left-side workspace pane, create a new directory called `templates` under `cloud9` directory. Create a new file named `temperature.html` inside the `templates` directory. The total path of this newly created file will be `/var/lib/cloud9/templates/temperature.html`. Write the following code in it and save:

```
<!DOCTYPE html>
<html>
<body>
<h1>{{temperature}}</h1>
</body>
</html>
```

This HTML file has no information other than declaration of variable `temperature`. This variable will get value at run time.

Create a **TMP36** sensor circuit setup like we did in *Chapter 5, Reading from Analog Sensors*. Click on the `cloud9` folder in the left pane to get back to the default `cloud9` directory. Create a new file with the name `flask_temperature.py` and write the following code in it. Save and run the program. Then open the web browser from your smartphone/computer connected to same router your BeagleBone is connected. Put this address in the address bar: `http://<Beaglebone's IP address>:3002`. You should be able to see the temperature value. If you touch the TMP36 sensor for a few seconds and refresh the page, you should see an increase in temperature. The code for `flask_temperature.py` is as follows:

```
import Adafruit_BBIO.ADC as ADC
from flask import Flask, render_template, request
app = Flask(__name__)

ADC.setup()
tmp36 = 'P9_40'

@app.route("/")
```

```
def print_temperature():
    volts = ADC.read(tmp36)* 1.8
    temperature = (volts * 100) - 50
    print(" Current Temperature is " , temperature)
    return render_template('temperature.html', temperature =
      temperature)

app.run('0.0.0.0', 3002)
```

Explanation

In our Python program we imported `Adafruit_BBIO.ADC` because we need to read from the TMP36 analog sensor. We imported the class `Flask` and some other functionalities from the module `flask`. Then we created an instance of this class. We provided the parameter `__name__` which is the name of the application's module or package. Using the `__name__` parameter allows this program to be used as an application as well as being importable in another application.

We used the `route()` decorator to tell Flask which URL should trigger the function defined next. The `route('/')` command means only website address without specifying any HTML file. So when the BeagleBone IP address (without addition of any HTML file) is entered in the web browser, it will call the function `print_temperature()` in our program. This function is similar to the temperature printing program we did in *Chapter 8, Physical Computing in Python*. We called the function `render_template()` which will load `temperature.html` and update the variable `temperature` in that HTML file with the current temperature we read from `tmp36`.

The last line `app.run()` actually runs our application on port `3002` and makes it accessible to `0.0.0.0`, which means to any IP address. When the remote web browser opens the BeagleBone IP address with the correct port, it internally executes the HTTP command `GET` for page `/`. Our web server application calls the `print_temperature()` function and responds to it.

Troubleshooting

Following are some troubleshooting techniques:

- Check the HTTP return code that gets printed on the console. This code reveals important information about communication, for example the return code `404` means page not found. Most likely you entered the wrong URL.

- For almost all errors, Flask returns **500 – server internal error**. Even wrong data type errors result with the same error. Printing variables locally might help you to guess which line is has the error. Please make sure the `temperature.html` file exists inside the `templates` directory.

- Add the parameter debug=True to the function app.run() for further debugging. Do not forget to remove the parameter when debugging is done. The app in debug mode which is exposed to the Internet brings security vulnerabilities.

- When you run this program multiple times, it may happen that an old Flask server that you ran earlier is still running. In that case, it causes a problem to start a new server on the same port. You will get the error **Address already in use**. You can find out the pid of an older process instance using the command ps aux | grep flask. Then you can kill it using the command kill -9 <pid>.

A program to control an LED through a web browser

Let us write a program to turn an LED connected to BeagleBone ON and OFF via a web browser. You can replace the LED with a buzzer to control sound remotely or with a relay to control AC devices. Here the web browser needs to send web server information if it wants the LED to be ON or OFF. So, the HTTP command GET is not useful. We will use the HTTP command POST here to send information to the Flask web server. Create a new file in the templates directory. Write the following code inside and save it as led.html. This file has two buttons which use the POST method to send information state = on or state = off to the Flask application. The code for led.html is as follows:

```html
<html>
<body>
<h1>LED</h1>
<form method="post">
<input type="submit" name="state" value="on" />
<input type="submit" name="state" value="off" />
</form>
</body>
</html>
```

Create an LED circuit setup like we did in *Chapter 3, Blinking External LEDs*. Create a new file with the name `flask_LED.py` inside the `cloud9` directory and write the following code in it. Save and run the program. Then open the web browser from your smartphone/computer. Put this address in the address bar: `http://<Beaglebone's IP address>:3002/led.html`. You should be able to see `on` and `off` buttons. If you press the `on` button, the LED should turn on. If you press the `off` button, the LED should turn off. The code for `flask_LED.py` is as follows:

```python
import Adafruit_BBIO.GPIO as GPIO
from flask import Flask, render_template, request
app = Flask(__name__)

led = "P8_10"
GPIO.setup(led,GPIO.OUT)

@app.route('/led.html', methods=['GET','POST'])
def change_LED_state():
    if request.method == 'POST':
        current_state = request.form['state']
        print current_state
        if (current_state == 'on'):
            GPIO.output(led,GPIO.HIGH)
        elif (current_state == "off"):
            GPIO.output(led,GPIO.LOW)
    return render_template('led.html')

app.run('0.0.0.0', 3002)
```

Explanation

In this program, the `route()` decorator specified that if the requested URL is `led.html` then we are interested in handling the method GET and method POST. This decorator will trigger the `change_LED_state()` function. Inside the `change_LED_state()` function, we are checking if the requested method is POST. If yes, then we collected the value of `state` from the template HTML file. If the value is `on`, we turn on the LED by the usual Adafruit BBIO method. If the value is `off`, we turn off the LED. In the end, we loaded the `led.html` page again irrespective of whether the method was GET or POST. Now, we can control the LED connected to BeagleBone from the remote web browser.

Troubleshooting steps for this program are the same as the last program. You can use a web browser Firefox extension **Poster** to create custom POST requests in GUI. You can also use the popular Linux command `curl` to create custom POST requests for debugging. For more details, check the manual page of curl.

A RESTful web app to control servo motor

Representational state transfer (REST) is a software architecture style of the **World Wide Web (WWW)**. This architecture is a set of constraints—client-server, statelessness, cacheability, layered system, code on demand, and uniform interface. These constraints improve the performance and scalability of web applications. For more details on REST architecture, refer to the following link:

```
http://www.ics.uci.edu/~fielding/pubs/dissertation/rest_arch_style.
htm
```

Once BeagleBone is connected to the Internet, it can communicate with servers on the Internet using protocols. Different protocols are defined to transfer different types of data. For example, the HTTP protocol was made for transferring and rendering HTML files. The SMTP protocol transfers e-mail. The SSH protocol gives a remote shell. Many online servers provide APIs to access their services via programs. Often this is done using custom protocol. If you want to access these services, there is a need for coding to call those APIs, for example Twitter provides APIs to access Twitter via an application. This is custom protocol implementation. This may or may not involve implementation of REST constraints. In our previous exercises, we did not follow REST constraints.

Another way of providing a web service is to use existing protocol. The most common protocol of the web is **HTTP**. It follows almost all the constraints of REST. So, if we implement our API over HTTP with uniform interface, we will be able to get the benefits of REST as standard. In that case, all our custom API request-response will be done over HTTP protocol. HTTP protocol has limited methods that can be called: GET/PUT/POST/DELETE. The standard way is to implement different APIs based on different resources. Each resource has a unique **Uniform Resource Identifier (URI)**. Some URIs are reserved for API communication instead of a HTML page. When the HTTP method is called on these URIs, an API response is given instead of an HTML page. Actions are performed based on location requested, for example if the client calls the POST method on URI http://api.example.com/member1/item17, the server will create Item17 as a new entry for member1. URIs are arranged in a uniform hierarchical way so that they are easy to manage. Learning different URIs is easier than learning custom APIs. Porting to other languages and platforms becomes easier as you are accessing HTTP links only. Also, you do not to have special software for testing. You can execute a few APIs from the client web browser. This will be clearer when you go through the next exercise. REST uses fewer resources, which is important for embedded systems.

Many popular IoT web services provide REST APIs to access them. We are going to use one such a web service later in this chapter. Let's write a small program that will provide a REST API to a client. If a remote web browser calls `http://<beaglebone IP>/servo/angle/<number>`, then it should change the angle of the servo motor attached to BeagleBone. There is no HTML file needed for this exercise. Attach a micro servo motor like we did in *Chapter 6, PWM – Writing Analog Information*. Create a new file with the name `flask_servo.py` inside the Cloud9 IDE and write the following code in it. Save and run the program. Then open the web browser from your connected smartphone/computer. Put this address in the address bar: `http://<Beaglebone's IP address> :3002/servo/angle/90`. You should be able to see movement in the servo motor and the text **angle changed to 90** appears in the web browser. You can try any angle between `0` and `180`. The code for `flask_servo.py` is as follows:

```python
import Adafruit_BBIO.PWM as PWM
from flask import Flask, render_template
app = Flask(__name__)

servo = "P9_14"
PWM.cleanup()
PWM.start(servo, 0, 60)
duty_min = 3

@app.route('/servo/angle/<angle>')
def change_angle(angle):
    angle = float(angle)
    print angle
    if (angle < 0) or (angle > 180):
        return "Invalid input"
    print (angle * 0.064) + duty_min
    PWM.set_duty_cycle(servo, (angle * 0.064)+ duty_min)
    return "angle changed to " + str(angle)

app.run('0.0.0.0', 3002)
```

Explanation

We used servo motor handling code the same as we did in *Chapter 8, Physical Computing in Python*. Our Flask app accepts the web address path `/servo/angle/<angle>`. This is our REST API URI. The inside function associated with this location takes the `<angle>` variable as a parameter. Then we apply our servo motor handling logic and return a string `angle changed to <angle>` which appears in the web browser.

We are not loading the HTML page first and then using any button/link to call our code. When we put `http://<Beaglebone's IP address> :3002/servo/angle/10` in the address bar of the web browser and hit *Enter*, control goes to `change_angle()` function inside our code with `10` as the parameter. Function `PWM.set_duty_cycle()` changes the micro servo motor shaft to angle `10`. Thus we can control the motor angle remotely. This exercise can be used in controlling the remote robot movement scenario.

You can combine the last three Flask programs with common lines removed and get all the exercises working at the same time on different web pages. In that case if you specify the BeagleBone IP address in the remote browser, you will get the temperature. You will be able to control an LED if you have visited `led.html`. You will be able control the servo by specifying the `servo/angle/<angle>`.

A program to trigger an e-mail alert on over-temperature

This is the same exercise that we did in *Chapter 7, Internet of Things with BeagleBone*. The Python package `flask-mail` can be used to create a local mail server inside BeagleBone to send e-mails. But to match the same example we did in *Chapter 5, Reading from Analog Sensors* we will use Gmail. An Internet connection is essential for this exercise. It is recommended to create a new temporary Gmail account for this exercise. You will have to visit the webpage `https://myaccount.google.com/security` and turn on **Allow less secure apps**. If you have enabled two-factor authentication, you will have to generate an *app password* from the same webpage. An in-depth explanation about this is covered in Chapter 7 for the same over-temperature exercise.

Create a circuit setup the same as we did for temperature sensing using TMP36 in *Chapter 5, Reading from Analog Sensors*. Open Cloud9. Write the following program. Change the e-mail addresses and password at the beginning of the program. Then save it as `emailAlert.py` and run it. Touch TMP36 with semi-hot metal and you should hit the 50 degree Celsius threshold. Then check if you got an e-mail at the e-mail address you specified in variable `emailTo`. If you are using an e-mail provider other than Gmail, you will have to change the variables `emailServer` and `emailServerPort` accordingly. The code for `emailAlert.py` is as follows:

```
#!/usr/bin/python

import Adafruit_BBIO.ADC as ADC
import smtplib
from email.MIMEText import MIMEText
```

```
import time

tmp36 = "P9_40"
check_interval = 4
threshold = 50
emailFrom = "xxxx@gmail.com"  ##gmail address
emailPasswd = 'yyyyyy'  ##gmail {app} password
emailTo = "zzzz@yahoo.com"  ## email address where emails will be sent
emailServer = 'smtp.gmail.com'
emailServerPort = 587

ADC.setup()

while True:
    time.sleep(check_interval)   ## wait 4 seconds to measure again
    volts = ADC.read(tmp36)* 1.8
    temperature = (volts * 100) - 50
    print " Current Temperature is " + str(temperature)
    if (temperature>threshold):
        msg = MIMEText("Current temperature is " + str(temperature))
##email body
        msg['From'] = emailFrom
        msg['To'] = emailTo
        #msg['Reply-to'] = emailFrom
        msg['Subject'] = "Overtemperature Alert!!!"
        server = smtplib.SMTP(emailServer,emailServerPort)
        server.ehlo()
        server.starttls()
        server.ehlo()
        server.login(emailFrom,emailPasswd)
        server.sendmail(emailFrom,emailTo,str(msg))
        server.close()
        print 'Email sent'
        time.sleep(3600)   ##wait 1 hour if email is sent
```

Explanation

We imported the module `smtplib` to use the `SMTP()` function. We also imported the `MIMEText` (**Multipurpose Internet Mail Extensions**) part of the module `email`. It is e-mail format standard. The first part of this program is very similar to a program that prints the temperature, which we have seen in *Chapter 8, Physical Computing in Python*. It calculates temperature. If the `temperature` is greater than the `threshold` value, it sends an e-mail. We first crafted an e-mail message with appropriate e-mail addresses, subject and e-mail body in mime format. Then we created an SMTP connection to Gmail server `smtp.gmail.com` on port number `587`. We changed the connection mode to **Transport Layer Security** (**TLS**). All SMTP commands and data will be encrypted here onwards. Here authentication is done with an e-mail ID and password. Then we sent an e-mail that we crafted earlier. Finally, we closed the SMTP connection and sleep for `3600` seconds (1 hour) before starting the temperature measurement again to avoid too many e-mails. Please note there is limit of how many e-mails you can send in a day. If you send too many e-mails in a short time, you will be blocked. This program can be combined with the push button program in *Chapter 8, Physical Computing in Python* to allow us to send e-mails by button presses.

Troubleshooting

Following are some troubleshooting steps:

- If you get the error **Name or service unknown**, then check if your Internet connection is working
- If you suspect a problem with the SMTP connection, turn connection debugging on by adding a new line `server.set_debuglevel(1)` before calling `starttls()`

Upload server data on cloud and visualize

Now that we can capture sensor data and get it remotely, how about generating graphs over the time to identify patterns and trends in sensor data? As BeagleBone is complete Linux system and has many database alternatives, sensor data can be stored locally and can be analyzed. But this needs a database and some other software set up. There are many free cloud services that provide this service for free for small data, for example Xively, ThingSpeak, Carriots, GroveStreams, and so on. These services collect, store, analyze, visualize, and allow you to share sensor data. Often they allow us to automate action based on data. All we need to do is store data on these severs periodically and view the graph on their website.

Let's use a popular IoT service, ThingSpeak, to visualize temperature data collected by our BeagleBone. ThingSpeak provides REST APIs. It collects sensor data sent through HTTP queries and graphs them in real time. This needs a ThingSpeak account. Visit the website `https://thingspeak.com/users/sign_up` and create a new account. ThingSpeak calls a data stream from one sensor as a field. Multiple fields form one channel. Each channel has a read and write API key. These keys provide access to get/set data on a channel. You need a write key to update data. Create a new channel with any name and description. Go to the **API Keys** tab and note down the **Write API Key** for that channel.

Attach TMP36 like we did in *Chapter 5, Reading from Analog Sensors*. Create a new file with the name `thingspeak_temperature.py` inside the Cloud9 IDE and write the following code in it. Change the API key in the program with the write API key you noted down earlier and run the program. The code for `thingspeak_temperature.py` is as follows:

```python
#!/bin/env python
import Adafruit_BBIO.ADC as ADC
import httplib, urllib
import time

tmp36 = 'P9_40'
update_interval = 20
my_key = 'XXXXXXXXXXXXXXXX'  ##Put your api key here

ADC.setup()

while True:
    volts = ADC.read(tmp36)* 1.8
    temperature = (volts * 100) - 50
    print " Current Temperature is " + str(temperature)
    params = urllib.urlencode({'field1' : temperature,'key': my_key})
    headers = {"Content-type" : "application/x-www-form-
urlencoded","Accept" : "text/plain"}
    conn = httplib.HTTPConnection("api.thingspeak.com:80")
    conn.request("POST", "/update", params, headers)
    response = conn.getresponse()
    print response.status, response.reason
    conn.close()
    time.sleep(update_interval)
```

Visit the link `https://thingspeak.com/channels` OR click on the button **Channels | My Channels** in the website to see your channels. Select the channel whose API key you used in the program. You should be able to see chart like this. This chart is customizable. You can do so by clicking the button on the upper-right side of the chart. You can set the minimum/maximum value to be considered. You can specify how many values it should show in the chart and so on:

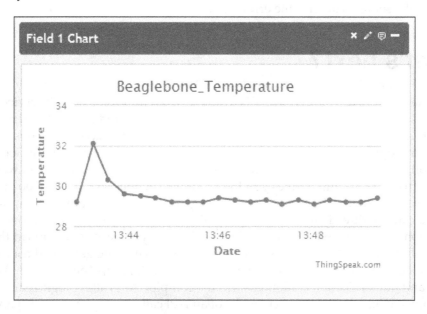

You can post this chart on your blog/website embedding code provided when you click on one of the upper-right buttons of the chart. You can share this chart by making your channel public. You can also link your Twitter account to send tweets based on data. ThingSpeak has an integrated MATLAB engine. You can do further mathematical analysis of data using MATLAB code.

Explanation

If you look at the total code, you can guess easily that this code is making an HTTP request. We are making a POST request to RESTful `api.thingspeak.com:80/update` with the content inside being *api key* and *temperature* data. ThingSpeak also allows you to import/export data in **Comma Separated Values (CSV)** format.

We included `httplib` and `urllib` modules to create a custom HTTP request. We did our temperature reading first like we did in *Chapter 8, Physical computing in Python* to print temperature. Then we created a custom HTTP header and parameter. We called a `POST` request on `api.thingspeak.com:80/update` with the header and parameters we just created. Then we collected response status code and status information. If everything gets executed correctly, the server sends the response **200 OK**. If there is an error, the server will send the error status.

What's next?

There are many platforms, like ThingSpeak, that allow uploading and analyzing sensor data. There are numerous APIs available from hundreds of web services. It is not possible for a developer to remember all these APIs and how to use them. A web service called **Temboo** addresses this problem. It allows access to thousands of APIs from popular web services in a uniform way. These services include Google, Microsoft, Amazon, Facebook, Twitter, GitHub, etc. You need to select API web services from the list and it gives you the setup instructions so that Temboo gets secure access to that web service. Then it can generate code in many languages that you can use directly inside a *thing* to call that API. Temboo supports code generation in Python and JavaScript. On BeagleBone, you need to download the Temboo Python and JavaScript SDK and then you can execute generated code inside BeagleBone. This generated code is very small code calling up Temboo with API details and authentication credentials. All the complex API calling logic remains on the Temboo cloud. You get direct results of an API call. So, it saves lots of space and computational power of a *thing*. Using Temboo, a basic IoT app can be developed without writing code. For more information, visit: `https://temboo.com`. There are similar but high level services available called IFTTT and Zapier. They allow you to create a relationship between various web platforms using GUI. You can automate a task in such a way that in particular conditions, your task gets triggered. For example, create a new note in Evernote when you star any message in Gmail, pause irrigation system automatically if rainfall is predicted by a weather website, and so on. Visit `https://ifttt.com/` and `https://zapier.com/` for more details.

We worked a lot on BeagleBone connecting to us and online services. We did not cover connectivity with other *things*. This is also called **Machine to Machine (M2M)** connectivity. A sensor network can be formed using M2M standards. For very lightweight embedded systems, even the HTTP protocol becomes heavy. There are many lightweight messaging protocols that exist that give security, **Quality of Service (QoS)**, reliability and other benefits to lightweight embedded *things*. Examples of such protocols are **MQ Telemetry Transport (MQTT)**, **Constrained Application Protocol (CoAP)**, **Extensible Messaging and Presence Protocol (XMPP)**, and so on. These protocols are suitable for IoT/M2M applications.

Security

We learned that the IoT has brought a whole new wave of possibilities. It brought a new wave of security concerns as well. IoT devices are connected all the time. That makes them even more vulnerable than desktop systems. A security bug can allow an attacker to take control of *things* remotely anywhere in the world. An attack might remain unnoticed for a long time. As these devices are working with the physical world, some damages can be catastrophic. The IoT is at an early stage and not many security standards are available. Security is an ongoing process. There is no complete secure point that can be achieved. Covering all aspects of IoT security will become a big book in itself. Let us see a few points that will make *things* more secure:

- Security vulnerabilities get discovered. Upgrade at OS and application level is important. BeagleBone comes pre-installed with stable Debian with a security repository enabled in /etc/apt/sources.list. You need to run the command apt-get update && apt-get upgrade to upgrade all the security-fixes. Do not install software from untrusted sources.

- Often services have configuration files that allow modification of security parameters, for example /etc/ssh/sshd_config has a configuration option to disable root login via SSH.

- Open only required ports needed for your work. On BeagleBone you can find open ports by running the command nestat -plntu. Don't use weak protocols like Telnet, **Universal Plug and Play** (UPnP). Use a firewall with the correct rules.

- Keep an eye on your data. Avoid data transfer and storage in plain text. Use encryption wherever possible. Use **virtual private network (VPN)** whenever possible.

- Do not use root login unless necessary. BeagleBone gives root access without a password. You should set a strong password for a root account. The default password for non-root users should be changed. Limit sudo access to a few commands only.

- Secure your local network. Anybody inside the network can open the bone101 page and Cloud9 with a root shell. Use a strong Wi-Fi password. Change the default router admin password. Use strong encryption for Wi-Fi. Limit your Wi-Fi range only to cover the longest connected device in LAN.

- Prevent physical access. Serial and **Joint Test Action Group (JTAG)** access can be possible with physical access. On BeagleBone, physical access allows you to copy/manipulate files on a SD card as well as onboard **embedded MultiMediaCard (eMMC)** storage.

- Create a failover plan. Make frequent backups.

Please note that these are good security practices. This does not guarantee your *thing* will be completely secure.

BeagleBone Black has dedicated bugs page here: `http://bugs.elinux.org/projects/beaglebone-black/issues`. To learn more about security on Debian, visit `https://www.debian.org/security`.

Summary

This chapter was about implementing the IoT using Python programs. We made BeagleBone connected components available on the Internet. First we made a web app that was showing temperature read by BeagleBone. Then we used the POST method to turn an LED attached to BeagleBone on and off remotely. We found REST is a popular standard for implementing the IoT. So, we created a small restful app that changes the angle of the servo motor based on the value provided in the URL. We wrote a program to auto-shoot e-mail when BeagleBone detects a temperature above the threshold. Then we looked at free cloud services to store, analyze and visualize sensor data. We wrote a program to store and visualize our temperature sensor data on the cloud service ThingSpeak. This concludes the book. We will see some important short topics in Appendices.

GPIO Control in Bash

We used JavaScript and the Python language in this book. You do not always need to write complex programs to control GPIO. You can access GPIO using simple BASH shell commands. You will need to use the sysfs interface for this; sysfs is a virtual filesystem created by kernel to export information and control of subsystems and hardware devices. So, if you modify the control files in this filesystem, you change the actual hardware parameters.

Check the BeagleBone GPIO map diagram that we studied in *Chapter 3, Blinking External LEDs*. It has the mapping of pin numbers with GPIO names. The P8_10 pin is the GPIO pin with number 68. It is given as gpio2[4] in the BeagleBone System Reference Manual. This means that P8_10 is the fourth pin in the gpio2 bank. The BeagleBone processor has four banks of 32 GPIO pins each—gpio0, gpio1, gpio2, and gpio3. Numbers 0-32 are given to gpio0 and 33-64 numbers are given to the gpio1 bank. So, the fourth pin in the gpio2 bank is actually the 68th GPIO pin. Thus, P8_10 gets converted to GPIO number 68. This conversion works for all the GPIO pins. We will need this number when dealing with GPIO on BASH.

Attach an external LED to P8_10 as we did in Chapter 3 for the blinking exercise. Write this shell program in Cloud9 or use the vi editor. Save it as blink.sh and run it from the Cloud9 IDE or in the shell using the sudo chmod 755 blink.sh; sudo ./blink.sh command:

```sh
#!/bin/sh
echo 68 > /sys/class/gpio/export
echo out > /sys/class/gpio/gpio68/direction
while(true)
do
    echo 1 > /sys/class/gpio/gpio68/value
    sleep 1
    echo 0 > /sys/class/gpio/gpio68/value
    sleep 1
done
```

Explanation

First, we wanted to use `/bin/sh` to interpret this file. By default, the sysfs files for particular pins are not created until we export them. We echoed 68 to the `/sys/class/gpio/export` file. This is a request to kernel to export the control of GPIO numbered 68 to the user space. After this command, the `/sys/class/gpio68` folder gets created with the control files in it. Now, we can interact with these control files that will actually change the pin state. As we have attached an output LED to the `P8_10` pin, we set the direction to out. As regular GPIO steps, we have to set the direction of `P8_10` as output. Then, we can turn it on/off by writing `0`/`1` in the special sysfs file, `/sys/class/gpio/gpio68/value`. We created an infinite loop using `while(true)`, and in the loop, we write `0` and `1` to the sysfs file after a second. When we write `1` on this file, the LED attached to `P8_10` will turn on. After a second, we write `0` on this file, which turns the LED off. You can get more information in the kernel documentation of the gpio sysfs interface at `https://www.kernel.org/doc/Documentation/gpio/sysfs.txt`. This way of accessing GPIO is possible on any Linux system (including Android).

Troubleshooting

- Change the first line from `#!/bin/sh"` to `"#!/bin/sh  -x`. This will print the line from the shell script before executing it.

- You can get information about the current configuration of all the working GPIOs from the following file:

```
sudo cat /sys/kernel/debug/gpio
```

B

BeagleBone Capes

Consider a scenario where our electronics project prototyping is done and we are getting the expected results. Now we want to make a production device out of it. We need to remove the breadboard and jumper wires and create printed circuit board (PCB) with an equivalent circuit. This expansion PCB will connect to BeagleBone via the P8 and P9 expansion headers. It will work as a plugin daughterboard for BeagleBone. This type of expansion board is called a cape. A cape for BeagleBone is similar to what a shield is for Arduino. This naming suits it because it looks like a cape around the Ethernet port when plugged in. BeagleBone comes with less peripherals on the board. Capes extend the capabilities of BeagleBone to have extra peripherals such as an LCD, motor driver, or **Real-time Clock (RTC)**. Some capes transform BeagleBone into totally different products like Replicape converts BeagleBone into open source 3D printer. Popular capes are listed here:

- `http://elinux.org/Beagleboard:BeagleBone_Capes`
- `http://elinux.org/CircuitCo:BeagleBoardToys`

Four capes can be stacked on to BeagleBone. The BeagleBone **System Reference Manual (SRM)** has a full chapter dedicated to capes. It provides you with many guidelines when creating a new cape. Capes needs to have 32 Kbyte I2C EEPROM connected to P9_19 and P9_20 I2C pins. It should contain board information such as the board name, serial number, revision, and so on. This EEPROM also has the information to `autoconfigure` the required expansion header pins. I2Caddress 0x54 to 0x57 are reserved for a BeagleBone cape. If there are two capes stacked on BeagleBone that have the same address, there will be address conflict. So, I2C addresses should be configurable via a jumper or dips switch. Then, by changing jumper/switch, you will force cape to use another address.

BeagleBone Black shares some expansion pins with the HDMI and emmc chip. BeagleBone Green shares a few pins with the emmc chip. Any cape dealing with these shared pins cannot be used with these boards. Though HDMI and emmc can be disabled, the hardware chips are still present on the board and can create problems. Here is the Wiki page that has a chart of capes of BeagleBone Black:

```
http://elinux.org/Beagleboard:BeagleBone_Black_Capes
```

Software part that deals with addition/deletion/controlling capes is called **Cape Manager**. Cape manager is part of BeagleBone kernel. It can load device tree runtime which is called device tree overlay. Cape manager checks for cape at the time of booting. You can see that in early boot logs:

```
bone-capemgr bone_capemgr.9: slot #0: No cape found
```

On BeagleBone Black, emmc storage and HDMI appears as virtual capes. You can also enable/disable cape by kernel command line options. For more information visit `http://elinux.org/Capemgr`

C

Pinmux and the Device Tree

We covered BeagleBone Capes in the previous appendix. Configuring capes requires pin mux configuration. Here, we will explore what pin mux is and how it can be changed using device tree overlay. We will also see why the device tree is used in the BeagleBone kernel and how the device tree overlay changes it dynamically.

What is Pinmux?

Different embedded projects deal with different components. Some embedded projects conduct communication with analog sensors. Some projects apply the ON/OFF logic on LEDs/buttons. Some interface with devices on I2C / SPI / UART. These different components have different types of voltage, current, and protocol requirement. We cannot attach an I2C device to a pin that follows the protocol of the SPI bus. Also, we cannot attach an analog sensor to the GPIO pin. This means that we need to have all these types of pins available on the board so that we can do any embedded project. Some embedded projects need interfacing multiple such interfaces. This increases the need of pins available in the CPU. It is not possible to have that many CPU pins. Therefore, there is a need to share the functionalities of available pins. This functionality that shares multiple pins is called **Pinmux**. Each pin has a set of different modes that support connecting corresponding components. Correct mode for the attached component has to be selected by the user. These pins support multiple voltage and current levels. Voltage and current level of pin can be changed according to the mode selection. BeagleBone SRM lists the possible pin mux modes in the Expansion header pinout tables.

The BeagleBone pins can have maximum eight different modes.

You can see currently configured pin mode using this command:

```
sudo cat /sys/kernel/debug/pinctrl/44e10800.pinmux/pinmux-pins
```

You can use utility config-pin to change mode of any pin. Run the following command to get information about this utility:

```
sudo config-pin
```

What is the device tree?

Our desktop systems (X86) come with BIOS chip, which provides important hardware information required to initialize kernel. ARM, however, does not come with any such information. All hardware information has to be statically written in kernel source. This modified source code cannot boot other boards which are very different. This means once kernel is modified to boot BeagleBone, it can not boot other ARM boards. Modified kernel has to be maintained by the vendor. They are responsible to bring all Mainline kernel changes to their modified kernel. To address this problem, new hardware description specification was introduced. These hardware description data structures are called **Device Trees**. These hardware description files are provided at boot time to the kernel by the bootloader and kernel uses them to initialize itself. Code for all ARM boards can exist in kernel and you specify your board details while booting via device tree files. BeagleBone kernel team went a step further and modified kernel to allow dynamically loading of small device tree overlay. This can help us to enable/disable hardware runtime. For more details visit http://elinux.org/BeagleBone_and_the_3.8_Kernel. We used device tree in *Chapter 9, UART, I2C, and SPI Programming*, to enable SPI pins while interfacing Nokia 5110 LCD. Adafruit Python library that we used has device tree files in the overlays source folder. They load runtime to change pin configuration. Cape manager deals with device tree overlays. Many prebuilt device trees are available in /lib/firmware. List of Device tree overlays loaded currently can be viewed by the following command:

```
cat /sys/devices/bone_capemgr.*/slots
```

BeagleBone Black lists HDMI and emmc in output. Device tree for HDMI and emmc are loaded at boot time. You can disable this boot time loading and free up expansion pins related to them to interface more components. You can disable HDMI by uncommenting the following line in the /boot/uEnv.txt file:

```
##Disable HDMI
cape_disable=capemgr.disable_partno=BB-BONELT-HDMI,BB-BONELT-HDMIN
```

Index

Symbol

7zip
  URL 6

A

Adafruit BBIO library
  about 96, 97
  URL 96
Advanced Package Tool (APT) 5
ADXL345 sensor
  about 119
  reading 120
  reference link 119
  troubleshooting 121
AIN0-AIN6 56
analog components
  reading from 57, 58
  writing 69, 70
Analog I/O 56
Analog to Digital Converter (ADC) 56

B

BASH
  GPIO, controlling in 143, 144
  GPIO control, troubleshooting 144
BeagleBoards
  URL 2
BeagleBone
  connecting, to Ethernet over USB 8
  connecting, to Virtual Network Computing
    (VNC) 10
  direct connection, to keyboard 7
  direct connection, to monitor 7

  Ethernet over USB connection,
    troubleshooting 8
  Ethernet port, connecting 9
  Ethernet port connection, troubleshooting 9
  General Purpose Input
    Output (GPIO) 33-35
  hardware 2, 3
  Pulse Width Modulation (PWM) 68
  Python programming 96
  reference link 12
  serial connection 10-12
  setting up 7
  URL 93
  USB Wi-Fi adapter, connecting 9
  USB Wi-Fi adapter connection,
    troubleshooting 9
  Virtual Network Computing (VNC)
    connection, troubleshooting 10
BeagleBone Black (BBB)
  about 4
  URL 4
BeagleBone Green (BBG)
  about 5
  URL 5
BeagleBone White (BBW)
  about 3
  URL 3
blink external LED
  circuit, analyzing 38
  circuit, setting up 35-37
  programming 38, 39, 97, 98
  troubleshooting 39
bone101 page 12, 13
BoneScript
  about 19
  URL 93

bus 110-112
bus protocols 110-112

C

capes
  about 145, 146
  reference link 145
Cloud9 IDE
  about 14, 15
  source code, URL 14
Comma Separated Values (CSV) 139
Constrained Application
        Protocol (CoAP) 140

D

dance external LEDs
  circuit, analyzing 40
  circuit, setting up 40
  programming 99, 100
  programming, in both directions 41-43
dancing LEDs
  creating 26-28
  creating, in both directions 29, 30
Debian image
  installing 5, 6
device tree
  about 148
  reference link 148
digital components
  reading 46
digital I/O
  about 18
  digitalWrite() function 19
  pinMode() function 19
Digital to Analog Convertor (DAC) 66
duty cycle 66

E

e-mail alert
  sending, on over-temperature 89-92
  triggering, on over-temperature 135-137
  troubleshooting 93, 137
embedded MultiMediaCard (eMMC) 141
Enhanced Capture (eCAP) 68

Enhanced High Resolution PWM
        (eHRPWM) 68
Ethernet, over USB
  BeagleBone, connecting to 8
Ethernet port
  BeagleBone, connecting to 9
Extensible Messaging and Presence
        Protocol (XMPP) 140

F

fading LED
  circuit, setting up 70
  fade in LED, programming 71, 72, 104, 105
  fade out LED,
        programming 71, 72, 104, 105
Flask
  about 128
  installing 128
Flaskr
  URL 128

G

General Purpose Input Output (GPIO)
  about 32, 33, 56
  controlling, in BASH 143, 144
  features 32
  in BeagleBone 33, 35
  on BASH, troubleshooting 144
Google security
  URL 90

H

hardware, BeagleBone
  about 2, 3
  BeagleBone Black (BBB) 4
  BeagleBone Green (BBG) 5
  BeagleBone White (BBW) 3
Hello World program 15
HTTP 133

I

IFTTT
  URL 140

Indiegogo
URL 78
Integrated Development
        Environment (IDE) 1
Inter Integrated Circuit
about 118
reference link 118
Internet of Things (IoT)
about 79, 80
JavaScript package modules, using 93
need for 78, 79
properties 80
security concerns 141, 142
interrupts
push button, reading via 49-51

J

JavaScript package modules
for Internet of Things (IoT) 93
URL 93
Joint Test Action Group (JTAG) 141

K

keyboard
BeagleBone, connecting to 7
Kickstarter
URL 78

L

LAN
servo motor, controlling through 87
LED
controlling, with push button 53, 54
LED, controlling through web browser
HTML code 84, 85
JavaScript code 85, 86
programming 84, 131, 132
light dependent resistor (LDR)
about 103
circuit, analysis 62, 63
circuit, setting up 61, 62
URL 61
light intensity
checking 63, 64, 103, 104

M

Machine to Machine (M2M) 140
micro servo motor
circuit, setting up 73
program, for controlling 74, 75, 105, 106
Minitwit
URL 128
Model-View-Controller (MVC) 128
monitor
BeagleBone, connecting to 7
MQ Telemetry Transport (MQTT) 140
Multipurpose Internet Mail Extensions 137

N

node.js http server
creating 81, 82
HTML code 81
JavaScript code 81, 82
troubleshooting 83
nodemailer JavaScript library
URL 90
using 89
Node-RED
about 93
URL 93
Nokia 5110 LCD
text, displaying 123-125

O

onboard LED
blinking 22, 23
program, executing to blink 24
timer, adding 24-26
turning, ON and OFF 20, 21
Output Compare Register (OCR) 68

P

pdb (Python debugger)
URL 97
period 66
physical computing 22
pinMode() function 19
Pinmux 147, 148

Poster 132
printed circuit board (pcb) 145
Pulse Width Modulation (PWM) 66, 67
Pulse Width Modulation Subsystem
    (PWMSS) 68
push button
  button-state detecting,
    interrupt used 101, 102
  circuit, analyzing 47, 48
  circuit, setting up 46, 47
  LED, controlling with 53, 54
  reading 48, 49, 100, 101
  reading, via interrupts 49-51
push button LED circuit
  analyzing 53
  setting up 52
Python
  URL 96

Q

Quality of Service (QoS) 140

R

Real-time Clock (RTC) 145
Representational state transfer (REST)
  about 133
  URL 133
RESTful web app
  used, for controlling servo motor 133, 134
RNDIS driver
  URL 8

S

serial connection
  used, for BeagleBone 10-12
Serial Peripheral Interface (SPI)
  protocol 121, 123
server data
  uploading, on cloud 137-140
  visualizing 137-140
servo motor
  controlling, through LAN 87
  controlling, with RESTful
    web app 133, 134

HTML code 88
JavaScript code 88, 89
socket.io
  source code, URL 84
sysfs
  URL 144
  using 143
System Reference Manual (SRM) 145

T

Temboo
  about 140
  URL 140
temperature
  displaying, remotely 129, 130
  printing 60, 102, 103
  troubleshooting, to display remotely 130
ThingSpeak
  URL 138
Time Base Counter (TBCNT) 68
TMP36 temperature sensor
  circuit, analysis 59
  circuit, setting up 58, 59
  URL 58
Transport Layer Security (TLS) 137

U

Uniform Resource Identifier (URI) 133
Universal Asynchronous Receiver
  Transmitter (UART)
  about 113-115
  reading 115-117
  troubleshooting 117-119
  writing 115-117
Universal Plug and Play (UPnP) 141
USB Wi-Fi adapter
  BeagleBone, connecting to 9

V

Virtual Network Computing (VNC)
  BeagleBone, connecting to 10
virtual private network (VPN) 141

W

Web Server Gateway Interface (WSGI) 128
win32diskimager
  URL 6
World Wide Web (WWW) 133

Z

Zapier
  URL 140

Thank you for buying
Programming the BeagleBone

About Packt Publishing

Packt, pronounced 'packed', published its first book, *Mastering phpMyAdmin for Effective MySQL Management*, in April 2004, and subsequently continued to specialize in publishing highly focused books on specific technologies and solutions.

Our books and publications share the experiences of your fellow IT professionals in adapting and customizing today's systems, applications, and frameworks. Our solution-based books give you the knowledge and power to customize the software and technologies you're using to get the job done. Packt books are more specific and less general than the IT books you have seen in the past. Our unique business model allows us to bring you more focused information, giving you more of what you need to know, and less of what you don't.

Packt is a modern yet unique publishing company that focuses on producing quality, cutting-edge books for communities of developers, administrators, and newbies alike. For more information, please visit our website at www.packtpub.com.

About Packt Open Source

In 2010, Packt launched two new brands, Packt Open Source and Packt Enterprise, in order to continue its focus on specialization. This book is part of the Packt Open Source brand, home to books published on software built around open source licenses, and offering information to anybody from advanced developers to budding web designers. The Open Source brand also runs Packt's Open Source Royalty Scheme, by which Packt gives a royalty to each open source project about whose software a book is sold.

Writing for Packt

We welcome all inquiries from people who are interested in authoring. Book proposals should be sent to author@packtpub.com. If your book idea is still at an early stage and you would like to discuss it first before writing a formal book proposal, then please contact us; one of our commissioning editors will get in touch with you.

We're not just looking for published authors; if you have strong technical skills but no writing experience, our experienced editors can help you develop a writing career, or simply get some additional reward for your expertise.

Learning BeagleBone

ISBN: 978-1-78398-290-5   Paperback: 206 pages

Learn how to love and care for your BeagleBone and teach it tricks

1. Develop the practical skills that are required to create an embedded Linux system using BeagleBone.

2. Use the embedded Linux software to control LEDs on the BeagleBone, empowering you to create LED flash patterns.

3. A hands-on guide, supported by practical examples to integrate BeagleBone into your projects.

Mastering BeagleBone Robotics

ISBN: 978-1-78398-890-7   Paperback: 234 pages

Master the power of the BeagleBone Black to maximize your robot-building skills and create awesome projects

1. Create complex robots to explore land, sea, and the skies.

2. Control your robots through a wireless interface, or make them autonomous and self-directed.

3. This is a step-by-step guide to advancing your robotics skills through the power of the BeagleBone.

Please check **www.PacktPub.com** for information on our titles

BeagleBone Home Automation

ISBN: 978-1-78328-573-0   Paperback: 178 pages

Live your sophisticated dream with home automation using BeagleBone

1. Practical approach to home automation using BeagleBone; starting from the very basics of GPIO control and progressing up to building a complete home automation solution.

2. Covers the operating principles of a range of useful environment sensors, including their programming and integration to the server application.

3. Easy-to-follow approach with electronics schematics, wiring diagrams, and controller code all broken down into manageable and easy-to-understand sections.

BeagleBone Robotic Projects

ISBN: 978-1-78355-932-9   Paperback: 244 pages

Create complex and exciting robotic projects with the BeagleBone Black

1. Get to grips with robotic systems.

2. Communicate with your robot and teach it to detect and respond to its environment.

3. Develop walking, rolling, swimming, and flying robots.

Please check **www.PacktPub.com** for information on our titles